Everyday Gardening and Meditation

*A blade of grass
can be a path
to a n̶e̶w̶ ̶y̶o̶u̶.*

D1495304

Steve Kane

F*** It.
Get A Divorce

The Guide For Optimists

Steve Kane

Please visit us at

GetHappy.Life

Dedication

To my Mom, and everyone who helped me through.

Contents

Welcome

1. How to pronounce our name 11
2. FIGAD is an EPBOT 13
3. Why this is for optimists 15
4. Caveat emptor 19
5. Welcome 21
6. I ♥ marriage 25
   Exercise: Earth still turning? 33
7. Get happy 35
   Exercise: Get old 37

Mind

8. By the numbers 43
   Exercise: DIY research 49
9. Lawyers 51
   Exercise: The Big 3 61
10. Money 65
    Exercise: Life budget 75

Heart

11. Tradition 83
    Exercise: The Time Machine 89
12. Don't take the bait 91
    Exercise: Cut bait 99
13. Get over it 105
    Exercise: The Shit List 111

Body

14. Sex   117
    Exercise: The Libido Meter   129
15. Pruning   133
    Exercise: Imagine no possessions   143
16. Dating   147
    Exercise: There's an app for that   155

Soul

17. Kids   159
    Exercise: Playtime   169
18. Timing   177
    Exercise: Citizen you   187
19. Escape velocity   189
    Exercise: Imagine   195

So now what

20. So now what   201
    Exercise: De-rut   204

Additional resources

21. A Divorce Dictionary   209
22. Playlists for your breakup   231
23. In-flight entertainment for your breakup   243
24. A Breakup & Divorce Cookbook   265
25. About us   287

Marriage is the chief cause of divorce.
—Larry Gelbart

You never really know a man until you have divorced him.
—Zsa Zsa Gabor

Let me tell how hard marriage is. Nelson Mandela *got a divorce! He spent 27 years in a South African prison, got beaten and tortured every day for 27 years and did it with no problem. He got outta jail after 27 years of torture, spent 6 months with his wife and said, 'I can't take this sh*t no more!'"*
—Chris Rock

How to pronounce our name

I'm ambivalent about profanity. I've never understood why some words are taboo while others aren't. Why, say, "damn" is bad yet "darn" is harmless. And I've lived long enough to know: Today's obscenity is tomorrow's yawn. Does anyone remember that "piss" was in George Carlin's famous "Seven Words"? (Don't know what I'm talking about? https://youtu.be/kyBH5oNQOS0)

Still, as a consumer products creator and marketer, I admit to happily exploiting the attention-getting value of the artfully placed provocation. Hence my title.

But. To try to offend as few as possible, I hope everyone can join me in pronouncing the title here as:

Effit: Get A Divorce

And to those who defy my wishes and pronounce the title otherwise, well, darn you to heck.

FIGAD is an EPBOT

F*** It, Get A Divorce, or *FIGAD*, isn't a book, though you can consume it in that form. It's not a video blog but you can watch it. It's not a podcast though it's available as one. And it has all sorts of peripheral resources like recipes and playlists. So what is it, exactly?

Heck if I know. But I like names so I'll give it one:

It's an *EPBOT*. An *E*xperimental *P*rototype *B*ook *O*f *T*omorrow.

Of course, for this I owe a deep bow to that quintessential genius, Walt Disney, who, in 1966, coined the name "EPCOT" to describe his vision for an Experimental Prototype City Of Tomorrow, which he hoped to build at the then just-announced Florida Disney World. Sadly, Disney's amazing EPCOT dream was abandoned, replaced by the fun but hardly visionary amusement park of today. (Watch Disney's original EPCOT plan, here: https://youtu.be/r9d2FEAR2t4?t=4m24s)

And obviously, today's authors are already busy making their material available in many forms, books, ebooks, audiobooks, podcasts, TED Talks, whatever, and have been for years. And the whole idea of a "book" as multi-pronged information and entertainment platform was brilliantly developed decades ago by pioneers like Louise Hay, at Hay House. More recently, my friend Seth Godin has reinvented what is meant by "book," "publishing" and "media," several times over.

So in truth I'm not inventing much here, just shepherding ideas and things together and bolting on a name, EPBOT. Still, I think it's worth coming up with a new label, as tomorrow's creators soon stop thinking of long form works as "books" at all, and every writer, teacher, thinker or publisher will feel the need, and exciting opportunity, to produce an EPBOT, a diversified, interactive platform for ideas.

In any case... I hope you enjoy this one.

And of course, to get the full-on EPBOT experience, please visit us anytime online at GetHappy.Life

Why this is for optimists

F. Scott Fitzgerald famously said, "There are no second acts in American lives." He was a literary genius, but a relationship dummy. Or pessimist, anyway. Of course there are second acts in American lives. In *all* lives. As well as third, nineteenth and zillionth acts, too.

If you're an optimist, that is. If you optimistically reject that a few words—say, *til death do us part*—eliminate forever the chance to begin anew. Or that bad decisions, or ones that despite good intentions and efforts turned out poorly, are final.

No, optimists think unfortunate, even horrible, situations are natural, inevitable challenges in any well-lived life.

And when it comes to significant relationships, aren't we all optimists and risk takers? Or, don't we all at least start that way? If we insisted success be guaranteed, no one would ever get seriously involved. And marriage is the ultimate gamble—the willful ignoring of the unlikelihood that two random people make each other happy, or happy enough, for 50 or 60 years.

Only us hopeful, romantic optimists take that bet. And it's so worth it, one of the great times of any life. The exciting beginning of a meaningful, loving relationship, a core experience of being human.

But then, as things do, relationships evolve and change. And for some, not for the better. Bonds weaken and strain. Maybe there are good intentions, maybe not. But the connection withers. And doesn't recover. And that's so painful, so intense and demoralizing, it can overwhelm the basic optimism that motivated us in the first place. To where we forget we ever had it.

Sound familiar?

Think that's forever?

If so, sorry, you're in the wrong place.

But if there's an optimist somewhere inside you, even just one tiny glowing ember, welcome. Maybe this can be a bellows, an inner-engine restarter, a hopeful guide to moving on, and in a calm, amicable, even loving way. Minimizing hurt. And not just for you.

Many—most—marriages and serious relationships don't last a lifetime. They just... *don't*. But when that happens, here we don't mourn or seethe. Optimistically, we say, well ok, time to do a reality check. Recommit and dig in for another attempt at rebirthing the relationship? Maybe. But, maybe not. Perhaps it's time to gently, thoughtfully, caringly put things in order. And take loving care of others. Then go back to being that hopeful you, start fresh, search for happiness again.

That's what optimists do, right? Fall down but get back up, brush off and keep moving ahead?

Pessimists see a tough situation and think, life is what it is, why bother. Too much risk. Too much possible pain. Staying put in unhappy relationships, they end up on autopilot, alive but barely living.

But optimists see the tough situation and think:

F*** it, get a divorce.

F*** it, my life isn't over, my chances for reinvention and happiness aren't limited, I just need to figure out how to move on. I need to be cognizant and careful to avoid bruising myself and others and that's not easy, and no matter what people will get hurt and so will I, but still, it's time to change my life—my precious, ever evaporating, one-and-only life.

So, I'm going to.

Sound like you? Or a person you'd like to be, or be again?

Then this guide's for you, optimist.

Caveat emptor

If you feel you're in real danger or risk call 911. Get away to safety, ASAP. Don't take chances.

If your health is at issue, consult a doctor. Not a coach.

This is not therapy. I'm a big believer in professional counseling, but I'm not a therapist. Think you maybe need one? Get one.

This isn't a spiritual endeavor. I can't help you understand or relate to God or "the universe." I'm not sure Heaven or Hell exist. Or enlightenment. Or Nirvana. If you need a spiritual guide, find one. (And for my sake, I hope Hell doesn't exist.)

I don't know if *you* should break up. Only you can know that. But I do know unhappy relationships do not need to be prisons. You're free to go. And I know people in relationships that aren't working and may not work again can use help thinking things through, and understanding what it's like to move on. If that's you, welcome.

Welcome

We're living one of the greatest experiments in the history of humankind, to try to create what has throughout history been considered a contradiction in terms: the passionate marriage. We're asking so many things from one person. We're asking one person to give us what once an entire village would provide. And couples are crumbling under the weight of so much expectations. Very few people achieve marital bliss. A lot more are miserable from it. They think they're deficient.

—Esther Perel

Welcome.

If you're here, I assume you're in an unhappy marriage or other committed relationship, or someone you care about is, or you're not really sure how you feel about things and you're looking for a way to try to sort out complicated, confusing feelings.

That was me, too.

And that's why I started this work.

Creating a course like this is a new thing for me. I've got no prior professional experience in coaching or relationship advice. Previously I was a startup entrepreneur (you can check me out in the *About* section.) But a few years ago my marriage went sideways, and my ex and I both knew it, and we went through therapy and other avenues and ultimately made what we thought was the best decision, but was actually a horrible mistake:

We stayed together.

The result was a period of unhappy years, utterly *unnecessary* woe, followed by a much more difficult divorce—an *unnecessarily* painful one. And with hindsight, I ascribe that more wrenching breakup to our forced bottling up of our feelings and our *true* desire: to move on. But we stayed...

And that really got me thinking. About how nuts my ex and I were, to have done that. Why were we so foolish? We didn't start out that way. And let me tell you, right here: my ex is an awesome person, partner and parent. This isn't a blame game. Also, while eventually we became irreconcilably unhappy, before that we were more or less content for some 20 years. It wasn't a perfect union. (Does such a thing exist?) We had plenty of potholes and misfires. But by most conventional measures, we were a decent success. And as I said, we *knew* we'd reached the end, and even went to therapy to try to sort it out. So why couldn't we do the seemingly obvious, logical, beneficial thing? Why couldn't we just acknowledge *reality*? Apparently we both were suffering from, what? Delusion? Paralysis from fear or shame?

My divorce was several years ago. But I haven't stopped that thinking. And that's changed my life. Made me a different person. Better? I hope so, but that's not for me to judge. Different? Definitely. For I now want to devote a major part of my time trying to help people who are just like that previous me. To assist folks in unhappy relationships to at least know what their options are, how the process of unwinding things can work, which issues need to be considered and which ones don't, and how breakups may *feel*—euphoric and painful—along the way. And to offer a little reassurance: You're not alone. You're not a bad person. You're not a failure. You're just a wildly normal human. And if you feel stuck, trapped or unsure about an unhappy relationship, you have two perfectly good, workable options: Stay. Or, go.

<‎ ‹⊪›

You can consume the material here any way you wish. It's available as videos, podcasts, downloads, even a high quality paperback book. I suggest a sequence to follow, but you can navigate in any order. Almost all segments are followed by brief "Exercises," some abstract thought experiments, some very practical, but all conceived as a way for you to not just listen to me, but to start to listen to yourself, too. What do you really feel about this or that? Offered a simple, clear explanation of a plan you may have to make, map out what you might actually do. Finally, I offer a lot of what I call *Additional Resources*, readings, links, music and playlists, videos and podcasts that I hope will be informative and even fun. Breaking up is rarely party time, but it doesn't have to be a funeral—and for the sake of everyone involved, I believe it shouldn't be one. After all, sometimes when we're feeling blue or confused it's best to just crank up a good tune and dance like a nutjob.

In addition to my own personal experience, I cite a lot of other experts, counselors, quotes and media offerings. I hope you find them as useful as I do. But, while in my searching for others' wisdom I looked hard for other coaching or advice *specifically* for people who want to explore breaking up, I found basically none. Yes, there are millions of programs, coaches, whatever, that help people work harder and recommit, try to renew stale or unhappy relationships. But ones that say, *Come on already, maybe it's best to just break up and move on*? Few, if any.

So probably this is a first for you, too. And you're wondering, so where does this end? Where does it lead me? And leave me? Well, know one thing: I have no idea if *you* should break up. I don't know you. But hopefully this material will lead you to a place of greater knowledge and understanding about what *all* your options are, and how breakup stuff works and feels, and how to candidly assess your possible futures. And to really, really know: There's more than one.

Given the title of this work, you probably know what I think most people in unhappy relationships should do. But like I said I don't know you, so if you'll forgive the metaphor, in the end I have to leave you at the altar. Break up, stay put, do something, do nothing, that's up to you.

So what do you think? Check it out?

I ♥ marriage

I'm very in favor of marriage.

Straight, gay and otherwise.

I buy the "traditional values" view that marriages and nuclear families are essential to a successful culture, to creating a society that provides an optimal foundation for people, particularly kids, with the love, education and support humans need to try to pursue happiness.

And that view is more than just a totem—it's a fact, supported by science and empirical data.

But I also have an open mind about what *is* a "family," and what makes a family functional, best able to offer such foundations.

So I'm also *very* in favor of divorce.

Of people breaking up unhappy relationships.

I think the alternative—staying—is worse. For nearly everyone.

A successful family does not have to have two adults, let alone two "committed" ones. Or the same two adults for eternity. Or, well, anything in particular. Whatever works, works. We're homo sapiens, an unusually intelligent, resourceful species. We invent, explore and engineer the universe as our default setting. We can have successful societies and great lives and families whether we stay with one partner or not.

There, of course, I depart from some of the more strident notions about "traditional values." Most important, I don't care what culture, religion or history have to say about, well, much of anything. Call me crazy, but I prefer to make up my own mind. For example, I reject that marriage, or any form of lifetime couple-dom, is an end unto itself. That there's some ultimate reward or dignity gained through relationship perseverance. Instead, I buy the cliche—the definition of insanity is doing the same thing over and over, expecting different results.

I likewise reject that relationship persistence is a form of altruism. We can take care of others *and* ourselves. We can be selfless yet not deny our *self*—a unique organism with but one life, and complex emotions and thoughts that are not ennobled by denying them. Or by acting as though "sucking it up" makes us a more mature or better person. Or by turning from the world, persuaded that denying longings is more enlightened than acknowledging them.

Of course, I don't live in any time or culture other than my own, so I won't—I can't—judge too broadly. I acknowledge that, today and throughout history, most humans say, do and believe what they think is right at the time. But as I live here, and now, in what by most measures is a blessedly modern, liberal culture, I *will* be judgemental about that:

For modern humans "til death do us part" may be the dumbest oath ever.

I mean, *'til death? Really?* No matter how long we live? No matter how unhappy a person is? No matter how many indignities one may suffer?

Sorry, no.

F*** it, get a divorce.

It's not virtuous to suffer. No one gets into paradise based on how masochistic they are. It's not heroic to limit one's own potential—or let circumstances or others do so.

In truth, for some of us, "'til death" is an archaic, unrealistic pledge, *even as we say it.* We live in the modern world, getting more so by the nanosecond, and we know what that can mean to longterm relationships. So some of us say those words out of nostalgia for simpler times, or some aspiration to banish loneliness, but we *don't* say such things out of a belief that we won the lottery—that, somehow, we randomly met another human who's *so* right for us they'll make us content day in, and day out, decade after *decade.* We certainly hope and pray for that, but we also know that far too often time changes everything and everyone.

Now, I'm not saying we should abandon ship at the first sign of rough weather. On that, I am a *traditional* "traditional values" person. Functional relationships and families aren't received. They're manufactured, through continuous recommitment, honesty, communication, humility, self-awareness, and hard work—and a willingness to forgive, then forgive again.

So no, I don't think you should quit your relationship easily. You were happy the day you got hitched and for good reason—your partner is a good person who you loved that day, and on so many other days, and who loved you. It's absolutely worth it to work hard to sustain that blessed state, that flickering candle of human harmony.

But let's be real: Sometimes the candle flickers out. Actually, it does so quite often. And sometimes we run out of matches—one or both partners has irretrievably lost their basic emotional attachment. The candle is never getting relit.

So then what? Do nothing? While away what may be eons of remaining life in longing and resentment?

No.

F*** it, get a divorce.

It's ok to have not won the lottery.

More important, it's not only ok to want to move on from an unhappy coupling, it's normal and wise to do so. Our right to "life, liberty and the pursuit of happiness" doesn't end or get restricted when we pair off. Hopefully, that pairing is an exciting, core part of that pursuit, but if it turns out the relationship has stopped being fulfilling, no longer provides the comfort, security, inspiration—the love—which was our expectation when we entered it, then, well, *duh*. We really do only get one life. Why would someone who *can* move on, can start over, can return to the basic human quest for a little happiness, choose to *not* do so?

As you're undoubtedly thinking: *For all sorts of good reasons.*

Loyalty. Fear. Money. Kids. Inertia.

That was me and my ex, alright. And we made the worst decision: To be righteous. Hang in there. Dig deep. Persevere. Keep it going if not for ourselves then for the family, the kids, the image.

Whatever lofty words are used to describe it, truth is, it was *dumb*. And a path to hurt. Our marriage was done and we knew it. But we wouldn't face it. *We're not quitters. We're taking one for the team.* Even though "the team"—us and our kids—became happier as a result of our *divorce*, not the slog years. Our ostensibly noble motives were actually a pressure cooker, which made our ultimate break up much more painful than it would have been had we just been honest and said:

F*** it. Get a divorce.

What stopped us? We caved. To fear. Cultural pressure. Internal personal pressure. Anxiety over being perceived a failure. Of hurting the kids (a false fear, as you'll see.) And of course, we caved to inertia. The devil we knew. That *devil*.

By the way, please know, up front, emphatically: None of this is to blame or point fingers at my ex. She was—is—terrific. Charming, brilliant, loving, funny, generous. A great partner and parent. That's why I fell in love and married her. And despite many years and life changes she was still that basic, good, loving person. She still is. But even great loving people make that bad, keep-going decision, despite that after those many years, from dating to mating and marriage, kids, careers and all the rest... the thrill is gone. To put it mildly.

Now we're divorced, amicable exes and co-parents. Yay! But it sucked getting here. Expensively, awkwardly, destructively sucked, sucked, sucked and sucked. It *sucked*. And all because we were unwilling to just face reality and *decide*. To just deal with it. For the longest, stupidest time. And we paid the price.

But *you* don't have to.

F*** it. Get a divorce.

Let me tell you what this programs *isn't*:

It's *not* a textbook explaining arcane divorce issues. It's *not* a how-to manual for getting away with anything or besting anyone. It's *not* a bunch of tips on how to get more, give less or work the system. The premise here is, be amicable and generous regardless of circumstances. You're unhappy so end the unhappiness, but aim for the best possible split and new beginning. Get expert help, divide things fairly, leave kids out of it and don't do or say anything you may regret later—later arrives quickly and you don't want your old unhappiness haunting you.

Most importantly, this *isn't* a program where I pressure you to do what I think. Yes, I say what I think and lean on you a little. But only to try to help you *decide—what do you want to do*?

Is this you?

I made a commitment. For better or for worse. I can't just walk.

But I'm unhappy. And I have little certainty that'll change. Don't I deserve to try to be happy?

Divorce is failure. I'm not a quitter. I'm resilient. Dedicated. Failed marriages are for failed people.

But I'm exhausted. My relationship isn't satisfying anymore. It was hot but now it's cold. In truth, I don't even look forward to being with my partner. It's a chore.

But I need to be an adult. I made my choices. Who said long term relationships stay exciting? Actually, everyone says all relationships cool. I'm acting like a spoiled child.

But I miss intimacy. Holding hands and meaning it. Snuggling. Kissing. Pillow talk. And sex. I really miss sex. Is that wrong?

I know I shouldn't, but I do care what other people think. If my marriage fails, people will judge me. I can't handle that.

But I don't even have dreams anymore. I'm trapped. How can I stay in an unhappy place for so many more years? Decades!

But I don't even know what it's like to be single anymore. I'm a couple now. That's my identity. My social circle. My life.

But I'm missing out. Missing feeling life can be an adventure. I only get one life. Shouldn't I try to get as much out of it as possible?

Who am I kidding? I can barely manage life with my partner pitching in. How will I juggle work, parenting, money and housekeeping on my own?

If that's at all familiar, this program may be for you. It's a mix of the personal and practical—been-there-done-that reminiscences, plus some science and data, plus interactive exercises to help you start re-imagining your life in privacy and safety. How does one prepare for a breakup? What's it like to say, *It's over*? What happens next? And next? What are the hangovers? The emotional gauntlet we navigate *after* the breakup?

Spoiler alert, here's the whole enchilada: You want to go? Go. Unhappy relationships are normal. Messy lives are normal.

Trepidation and paralysis are normal. You're not alone. If you're guilty of anything, it's only of being human. No shame. You're off the hook. Free to do as you wish. You can reinvent yourself, over and over, and pursue happiness as you see fit. There's still time and opportunity. There's always time and opportunity. And with the right mindset and preparation, no one needs to get badly hurt. Breaking up is always a disruption, but it doesn't have to be a tragedy. And shouldn't be. The end result can be upbeat, a fresh start, a shedding of seething, resentments and unhappinesses, for everyone. In the end, it's *not* the end, it's a *beginning*, with relief and renewal, and not just for you.

So come join us other frail humans? All us reasonably well-adjusted, reasonably smart, reasonably functional folks who find ourselves in a rut, gripped by indecision, feeling isolated, hamstrung by anger, confusion, fear and shame? There's no magic remedy here but we'll breathe deep and mull over some of the issues involved with moving on from a longterm relationship. You're not obligated to do anything, except consider. Think.

And remember: There's no guarantee you'll make no mistakes, feel no pain. You will. Breaking up hurts. No matter what. It's one of the most profound life events, involving deep reflection, emotions running rampant, tempers flaring and people getting bruised. I wish I could save you from all that. But no can do.

Still, I say:

F*** it. Get a divorce.

I think for most of us the price is worth it. I think it's better to feel than to not feel. Which means life hurts sometimes. And avoiding hurt means avoiding *life*. Some years ago I was lucky to do work with the great life coach (and friend) Jerry Colonna. *My problem is I get too emotional about things,* I told Jerry, *I need to stop feeling everything so much. What should I do?*

Nothing. Jerry said. *You're human. An emotional being. That's what being human is. Turning off emotions is to be less human.*

Is that what you want? We all know people who've done that. Do you really want to be more like them?

I don't. So I embarked on a mission: To feel grateful for life itself. Hurts, indignities and all. It's a constant struggle. I fail often. When life sucks, it's hard to be thankful. But by at least trying, more living is possible. More opportunities. Because I spend less time brooding. It's not easy, but it's worth it. And the alternative—more anger and despair—is worse.

Ditto, unhappy relationships. Meaning, if we prepare ourselves, and try to stay focused on the positives, the hard breakup stuff can be lived more easily. Moving on needn't be a zero-sum game, with "winners" and "losers." With forethought, and basic gratitude for life, everyone can emerge with love and dignity. A break up is not a death. It's a *birth*. Painful and messy, but also something new and wonderful.

⟨⊞⟩

So. Here's your first Exercise. Say this out loud:

I'm in an unhappy relationship. I'm thinking about leaving. Which means I'm a normal, good person.

Earth still turning?

Get happy

Happiness requires the ultimate sacrifice: To give up one's unhappiness.
—Marty Rubin

Are you unhappy?

What is happiness? Philosophers, artists, preachers, therapists and gurus eternally ponder that, grasping for *positive* definitions, distillations of the essence of contentment.

Not me. I give up. The question's too neat. Happiness isn't a *thing*. It's a whimsy, a "know it when I feel it" ephemera. And each person's happiness is unique to them, evolving and changing moment by moment.

So then, *what the heck?* The main premise of this program is that we all deserve to seek happiness. And should do so. And so therefore, by definition, we should not stay in unhappy relationships. But if I can't even be bothered to say what happiness *is*, how dare I tell people to turn their worlds upside down, to go after it?

Easy.

See, here we rely on a *negative* definition of happiness. Meaning, I'm pretty confident I know what's it's *not*.

Happiness is *not being unhappy.*

I know, that's messy. But stay with me, I think it'll do.

I'm not going to try to convince you I know what happiness is for you. Or for anyone. But I am going to try to persuade you that we can best pursue happiness, whatever it may be, by eliminating people and things that make us *unhappy*.

And I daresay: We all know what *unhappiness* is. And we all know what it feels like when we manage to remove a cause of unhappiness from our life.

It feels good.

Or at least, it feels like relief. Like our inner balance scale, with happy on one side and unhappy on the other, is tilting just a wee bit more to the happy side.

For me, that'll do.

I mean, if I jab you with a pin, when you grab the pin away, you feel happy, not because grabbing the pin is a "happy" event in and of itself, but from getting rid of the poking. Imagine I wasn't jabbing you. Would you feel happy grabbing a pin away from me?

I know, it's not a shattering or novel insight. But I'll take it. Because it works here. Here, it doesn't matter that I don't have a clue what happiness *is* for you because if I *do* know you're in an unhappy situation, then I feel confident saying that eliminating *unhappiness* is a positive. It's just common sense.

Clear as mud?

1) I won't pretend I know how to make you happy.
2) If you say you're unhappy, I accept that you are.
3) I'll try my best to help you become less unhappy.

Deal?

<###>

By the way, this is not relationship therapy. Or personal therapy. The world is full of valuable and wise "fix your relationship" and "fix yourself" counsel. But this isn't that.

Probably, you're perplexed how you got from "there" to "here"— from delight and sex to tedium and texting. We blink and ten years have passed. What happened? Naturally, we want to try to understand. Just, not here. Relationships go sour in a million ways, but for our purposes, it doesn't matter how you got to an unhappy place. All that matters is, you're unhappy. And that, maybe that can change.

Yes, it does matter why your relationship isn't working or may never work again. Yes, it matters what choices you made, what you did well and poorly, and what you may be able to do better going forward by being more reflective and self-aware. But still, this isn't therapy. It can't be. I don't know you. And in any case, I believe that regardless of how one gets in a funk, the single most important step towards getting out is to be able to say, *I'm in a funk. And I want it to stop.*

It doesn't matter how you got there. You're in an unhappy relationship. And that's totally OK. And marriage is indeed a valuable, important institution. And commitment is essential to successful relationships. But it's no sin, no failure, to find oneself feeling unhappy to be bound to one human for an entire life. On the contrary, it's utterly predictable. Most couples today end up unhappy. In the modern age, it's just not reasonable to think two people will meet, randomly, then commit for life, then not come to regret that decision, ever, decade after decade. *Both of them.*

Of course, the decision to move on is a *huge* one, a literal life changer in every possible way. To even think about making such a momentous choice, maybe it's best to start small, carefully consider whatever factors should go into such a resolve. Say, like answering a basic question:

Are you unhappy?

Exercise

Of course, most people feel they are just one "me," just one person for their entire lives. But there's an interesting counter view: Actually, we're not just one person. The "me" of 20 years old is quite literally a different "me" at 40. And 60. Or wherever we place the age breaks. Consider: if the "you" of 20 met the "you" of today, would they agree on everything? Violently disagree on some things? Think the other one was an utter fool or even repugnant about anything?

For this exercise, try to imagine: What will make your "me" of, say, 20 years from now unhappy? Or happy?

And don't just imagine all this in your head. Make a visual aid. There are several, excellent, free smartphone apps that can eerily, accurately age your selfie pictures, showing what you will probably look like X years in the future. Download one of these apps. Age your own picture 20 years. Print out that "Future Me" picture, put it in a nice frame on your desk or someplace you see it often, and get in the habit of asking "Future Me": What are you unhappy about? How long have you felt that way? Was there anything I (now) could have done to make your life less unhappy?

There are many "make me look old" apps. Search "make me look old" on the Google Play or iTunes App Stores. Or here's one well reviewed app, Oldify: http://www.oldify.net

Mind

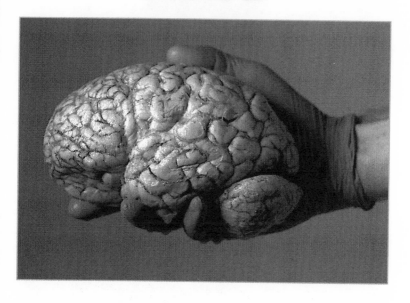

Facts are simple and facts are straight.
Facts are lazy and facts are late.
Facts all come with points of view.
Facts don't do what I want them to.

—Talking Heads
  Crosseyed and Painless

By the numbers

There are three kinds of lies:
Lies.
Damned lies.
And statistics.

—Mark Twain

You've probably heard the statistic: 50% of marriages end in divorce. There's debate about its accuracy (see Mark Twain quote) but there *is* broad agreement that some *huge* percentage of marriages break up.

Can such information aid *you*?

In the past there was little data to help us manage our lives. Tradition and social norms ruled. People felt pressure to conform. But now there's an ocean of science and data. The old pressures still exist but we no longer need scripture or scuttlebutt to gauge how we fit in. We can *know*, at least in a general sense.

But is that useful to *individual* lives and decisions?

I think, yes.

In 1996, psychotherapist and bestselling author of *Too Good to Leave, Too Bad to Stay,* Dr. Mira Kirshenbaum posited that 20% of people in relationships (all, not just marriages) are struggling with whether to leave. 20% is huge, but I assume it's low. Just as pollsters missed Trump's win because nobody would say they favored him, I believe few folks admit they're in relationship turmoil.

But even 20% should be heartening: *You're not alone.* You're in a big crowd. We're each unique but our struggles are common.

Plus, statistics shed light on *trends,* on where we're heading. A 2017 Gallup study found divorce "moral acceptability" at 73% in the USA, an all-time high and rising fast—up 14 points since 2001. Meaning, almost no one condemns breakups today and soon nobody will. So you can know: The anxiety you may feel about being poorly judged by others is at least partially imagined, maybe entirely so. The data shows: Almost no one around you condemns divorce, and it's lessening.

Even more reassurance comes from the trend data on how governments and laws are changing, making divorce easier:

> **During the last century all states changed the way they allowed divorce. In the 1970s alone, a "divorce law revolution" resulted in amendments to or repeals of divorce laws in 37 states. The new laws allow individuals to divorce under a "no-fault" system rather than under the previously restrictive, cumbersome fault-based system.**
> **Family Relations, *Vol. 51, No. 4, Families and the Law***

◄╫►

Specific data and numbers aside, I hope you can start to see the overall view is pretty clear: Breakups and divorces are common. Normal. And trend-wise, it's a virtuous circle—as these things become more widespread, less people care, which makes them become more widespread, which make less people care, which...

Well I hope you get the picture. And that that's useful to you, as an individual, now. You're not alone. You haven't flopped. Unhappy relationships aren't failures, they're ordinary experiences. Most important, in today's world you can stop feeling shame. Stop assuming the worst about what other people might think. Stop suffering. Start seeking contentment again. As you wish. You're not fighting the tide, you're surfing the wave.

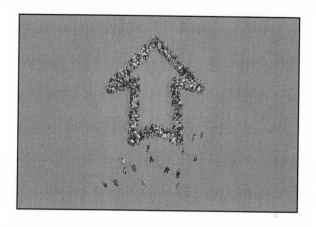

Talk to younger folks. They don't believe marriage is some fairy tale of continuous contentment. They know it's a romantic but risky bet. With high rates of failure. So they put off wedlock until they have better grasps of needs and finances (or maybe forever):

Half of Americans 18 and over were married in 2015, compared with 72% in 1960. Americans are staying single longer. In 2012, 78% of 25-year-old men had never married compared with 67% of females and by 2016, the median age at first marriage reached its highest point on record: 29.5 years for men, 27.4 years for women.
Pew ThinkTank: *5 Facts on Love and Marriage in America*

Young people today want romantic love but they know that rarely means eternal love. They don't walk down the aisle assuming marriage makes magic. Unlike previous generations, which basically dove into marriage with eyes closed and fingers crossed, today's younger crowd manages their own expectations.

You can too.

Try a thought exercise:

Imagine a future where marriage isn't "til death do us part." Where a marriage license is like a driver's license—it needs to be renewed, or it expires, say, every seven years. And the only way licenses renew is if both partners do so. If one partner doesn't, the marriage expires. Poof: Done.

Further, to get a license, partners sign contracts stating how much wealth they have and whether they're contributing that to the marriage or keeping it separate. And both agree new wealth acquired during the marriage is owned 50/50. So if the couple doesn't renew, no money fights. Likewise kids. If a couple doesn't renew, future law mandates 50/50 financial responsibility and custody and formulas determine compensation if a partner has to beg off. Ditto alimony and child support: No fights.

In other words, imagine a future where the major pressures of divorce—religious, social, legal and financial—are gone.

It's not so far fetched. Slowly but surely we're heading there. Check statistics about Europe. Fewer and fewer couples are marrying there. Why bother? Meanwhile, European divorce rates creep up...

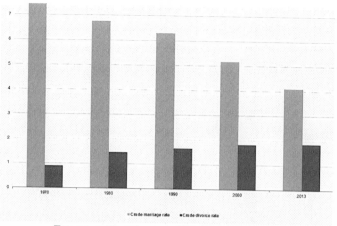

Eurostat: *Marriage and Divorce Statistics*

So. In that future world, how many couples marry for life? I think, almost none. Check out this recent U.S. Census statistic:

- 41% of 1st marriages divorce
- 60% of 2nd marriages divorce
- 73% of 3rd marriages divorce

Why does the rate increase in second and third marriages? Because everyone who has been divorced *once* knows a) fear of divorce is far worse than actually getting one, and b) when you exit an unhappy marriage you're *happier.*

Imagine a future where everyone knows all this from the get go?

I know, we're not there. And you're in a big, complex personal storm not a science fiction parable. But at least let the statistics hearten you: You're just a common *human.* As the data shows, the institution of marriage, and the perception and frequency of divorce have radically evolved. For the better. *Your* better. The tide is turning, in favor of more human liberation. Empowering people, making us free to keep trying to be happy.

Free to keep trying to be happy.

Imagine that.

Goodness, look at the date. Your marriage license has expired.

Want to renew?

Exercise

Do a little research of your own. But in a completely simple, safe, easy way: Acquire some data by talking with friends or colleagues. If possible, take notes.

If you need a cover story, say you're intrigued by something you read online: *Hey, I just read a crazy blog. It says in the future marriage licenses will be like drivers licenses—they'll have to be renewed or the marriage is over.* Then just casually chat about that.

Here are some other suggested research topics:

- How many *married* people do you know? How many divorced? Do the numbers come out roughly 50/50?
- Speculate: How many couples do you know who'll be together until death? How many do you know who you think will break up in the next few years? How many do you know who, break up someday or not, seem unhappy?
- Ask people: Is divorce wrong? Or no big deal? What's the percentage on each side? Is there a clear majority?
- Ask: Should unhappy married people stay together forever?
- Do a simple trends analysis. Ask: Did your parents think differently about marriage and divorce than you do? Were they more tolerant or more disapproving than you yourself are? And are your children more or less tolerant than you?
- Finally, ask divorced people: Do you regret your divorce? Do you ever wish you were still married to your ex?

Lawyers

*You can't get what you want
'til you know what you want*
—Joe Jackson

Lawyers *suck*.

Get one.

<hr>

Do you shudder at the thought of dealing with lawyers? That's understandable. Attorneys speak in jargon, so talking to them can be tough. They're highly educated specialists, so they can come off as arrogant. And they're expensive. And the legal system feels like a Rubik's Cube. So it's completely natural to be apprehensive. Still:

If you're in a bad relationship, don't let attorney anxiety keep you there.

Ending a longterm relationship is almost always a legal affair, so you need legal advice. It's that simple. Dealing with lawyers can stink, but the *worst* breakup experience lasts a year or so. Often less. Staying in an unhappy couple? *That lasts forever.*

Or maybe it's tempting to think, *I can deal with this. Divorces are fairly routine things. I'm no genius but I'm smart enough. And I've got Google.* Just like we can all fix our own cars and do the dentistry work on our kids? You're not a legal professional. You're in a highly emotional place. So don't negotiate your own deal. And if you somehow do end up bartering with your ex, make it clear such talks aren't final, everything's open to revision after an attorney can be consulted.

Then consult one.

And a quick word re: mediators.

They're awesome. Just don't depend on them.

The attraction of mediation is it's cheaper, faster and friendlier. While lawyers can be expensive, slow and antagonistic.

All true.

But the reason I say people shouldn't depend on mediators is exactly that: Mediators *aren't* advocates. They don't represent anyone. They're in the middle, taking no sides, which keeps things amicable and speedy, until later you realize: *The mediator didn't consider anyone's best interests.* If they're staying neutral, they can't. Their job is, get a deal done quickly—any deal that's legal. If someone says yes to a bad idea, ok. If an issue should be ironed out but the law says it can be ignored, ok.

Mediators may be good people and genuinely care about you, but they don't know you and they're not paid to wonder if things are good for you. They're not advocates, they're facilitators. If the parties agree to an awful idea or don't consider its ramifications, well whatever, mark and move, next question.

Which doesn't mean mediators can't provide great help. Good ones can create an amicable, get-things-done environment, hashing out minimums, avoiding spats. Just, never agree that deal is final. Require any final agreement to be reviewed by attorneys. If your ex chooses not to, that's their (dumb) choice. But you? *Talk to a lawyer.*

A lawyer is an expert advocate. *Your* expert advocate. With one job—representing your interests. Your deal is critical *now*, and also often impactful far into your future. No decent lawyer will let you agree to anything without first explaining what they think and why. And *how* they represent you is up to you. Maybe you say, get everything, give nothing, scorch the Earth. Maybe you say, get my fair share but no fights, keep us friends.

A close friend used a mediator for her divorce. He was smart and kind. Both my friend and her ex liked him. They finished quickly and inexpensively. The Judge signed the deal and presto chango: Divorced! Everyone was happy.

For a few months anyway.

Under their agreement, the ex-husband paid child support, partially funded as a percentage of his bonus pay (and partially funded as a fixed monthly amount.) But the deal only let her know once a year how much that bonus amount would be, at the time he handed over her percentage. She didn't mind because he only got paid his bonus once a year, and he'd had the same job forever and loved it, so she felt she knew roughly what to expect.

Then he got a new job. But he didn't tell her how much he was getting paid. Their deal didn't require him to. She pressed him but he'd only say his salary hadn't changed and a bonus hadn't been decided and could be zero. She asked for documentation but he refused, which was entirely his right. So now child support was maybe less than she thought she'd agreed to, maybe a lot less. But other than once a year, she couldn't know and even then it was just his word. He had no obligation to provide any documentation, ever.

It got ugly and painful, for months.

Finally, she got a lawyer. Who advised they had the legal right to contact his new company and request employment information. The lawyer also recommended they send the ex-husband a lawyer letter, explaining that if necessary the lawyer would haul him into court to explain himself to a Judge. Off went the letters. Which made the situation even more bitter. And my friend spent $1,000. And would have spent much more if they went to court.

But the company quickly disclosed the ex-husband's employment terms. And rather than gamble on the sympathies of a Judge, the ex-husband signed a new deal, guaranteeing transparency and certainty about child support.

And there in a nutshell is the problem with mediation. No one did anything wrong during mediation. They got a legal divorce agreement. No one violated it. But during negotiation, no one professionally looked out for anybody. A deal got done quickly but poorly, avoiding conflict today but lighting a fuse.

Lawyers have only one job: Protecting your ass. While it may cost you a bit, it will be money well spent.

So. Now that I've extolled the *virtues* of divorce lawyers, let me point out the by-far *worst* thing about them:

A divorce lawyer always has a conflict of interest with her client: The messier the divorce, the more money she makes.

You want the best possible deal, quickly, cheaply and with minimal hurt. But the slower and more difficult your divorce is, the more fees your attorney collects.

YUCK.

But so what. If you listen well and speak up, that conflict can be managed, minimized, even nullified. So no matter what, my message is the same: At some point in your breakup, get a lawyer. To educate yourself and—*at minimum*—review your deal before you sign anything. Again: If you're ending a relationship with legal issues (kids, co-owned assets, whatever) *you need legal counsel.*

Before I said: *Lawyers suck. Get one.* Now I'll add:

And *manage* her.

Before you even meet a lawyer, embrace a simple idea: *You* are the decider. Be a good listener and always consider your lawyer's view, but in the end decide for yourself what's best. And don't look back, don't second guess, just keep on to the next issue.

Say what you think even when you're confused. Or nervous. Which you will be. A lot. We all are. But so what. News flash: Sometimes you'll be wrong. So what. You'll do fine. No one can make decisions about your life better than you. And remember: Even Ted Williams, maybe the best hitter ever in baseball, only hit .406. Which means he *didn't* get a hit 6 times out of 10.

And never be afraid to talk fees.

It's your money. You have every right—and obligation—to try to spend it responsibly. Make sure your lawyer knows you're budget sensitive and what your limits may be. (And I don't care how wealthy you think you are—you're budget sensitive.) Or just say,

I know everything is subject to change, but ballpark guess, how much should I budget to work with you and get my deal done?

If they balk, walk. Any decent lawyer will be comfortable talking about how much things may end up costing, and why. They'll understand you have limits and if they think there's a problem, they'll say so. And if you're not OK with *that*, politely walk away and find another lawyer. *The world is full of them.*

If you don't like pressure and lawyers just plain make you feel intimidated, congratulations, that's normal. Just never forget:

You don't have to do anything because a lawyer says so.

You may want to. You may not. Take whatever time you want to make up your mind. And change your mind. Again and again. Everything's always your call, for one simple reason:

You're the boss. The lawyer is your employee. Not the other way around.

They're there to advise you, educate you, give you the benefit of their knowledge and experience, maybe even comfort and console you, but regardless, *they work for you.* And they know it, and they're good with it, because it's just the truth.

And if you *don't* take charge, you'll create a vacuum, and the attorney may fill it, assert control if for no other reason than if no one does, the deal won't get done. But then you get what the attorney thinks best, not you.

Also, if you don't take charge you risk getting rolled by your ex. Your attorney may cave on things because that's the signal your detachment sends: *I don't really care, just get it done.*

Why risk any of that when the solution is simple:

Speak up.

One of my oldest friends had an amazing career in Hollywood. For years he was a successful talent agent, representing big stars and directors. I was so impressed. Nothing in his education or background suggested that path so obviously he was a natural born genius at negotiation. So I asked him: *Teach me to be a great negotiator?* He just chuckled. *Easy,* he said, *Just tell people what you want.*

Meaning, almost no one does. Everyone's too nervous. Or thinks they have to be crafty or sophisticated. But great negotiators know: You stand a much better chance of getting what you want *if you just say clearly what you want.*

Ridiculously common sense? A consistent surprise in my life is discovering how few people do this. Most people go through life reluctant to articulate what they want in relationships, in work, in whatever—hoping, I guess, that other people read minds.

Breaking up is no time to pray for clairvoyance. *Speak up.*

I know, that's not easy for everyone. If being assertive isn't your natural disposition, or just speaking up can be a struggle, then maybe start off with a little work with a Divorce Coach. By now we've all heard of Life Coaches, professionals who don't just listen to our heart and soul baring like a therapist, but also actively talk back at us, offering advice or practical techniques for dealing with issues. Divorce Coaches are just Life Coaches with a very specific focus: Helping people prepare for and live through the challenges of a legal relationship breakup. Good ones are awesome—deeply sensitive, empathic and knowledgeable. And helping people identify what's important to them, and teaching how and when to speak up, is essentially their number job with any client.

When your deal's done, it's forever. A continuing, meaningful part of your life. But only for you, your ex and kids. The Judge and lawyers forget you instantly.

Own your deal *as it happens*, not just when it's done.

What *you* think, what *you* want, what *you* decide must reign supreme every step of the way. Lead from the front or from behind, but *lead*. If you screw up, whatever. You screw up. Perfection is the enemy of the good. Aim for the good. Fix mistakes when you can. Or just live with 'em. Don't think if you let something play out you'll still get more or less the same deal. News flash: your attorney barely knows you. And sometimes their work make them bleary-eyed: You're just another case. So sometimes they're on autopilot. Not because they're unethical, because they're *human*. You and I would be the same. So pay attention all the time, not just the end. Details can be tedious, weird and annoying. So what. *It's your life*. And your attorney's bleary-eyed-ness can be a huge help. Their addled brains are terrific libraries of how things usually work in real life. Always ask, *Have you seen this before?* The answer is often yes. Then ask, *How does it usually get resolved? Is the typical outcome so typical I may as well just go there and save time and trouble?*

But just because sometimes lawyers fall into autopilot doesn't mean you should.

⟷

Concerned your lack of knowledge will hurt you?

Don't worry about how little you know.

Welcome to Club Normal. Just never hesitate to say, *I don't understand, please explain that again.* If after hearing the explanation you're still not clear, ask again. And again. Until you *are* clear. (More ridiculously common sense almost no one uses.)

Ask tons of questions—especially ones you think are dumb. They're not. And if a question *is* dumb, who cares. It's your life we're talking about. Ask whatever you like, as often as you like.

⟷

Simple, huh?

Heck, no. This is scary. You're not a lawyer, you're not a business mogul who manages them routinely, maybe you've never handled anything like this before. And it's happening at the worst time—you're a mess.

But that's the point. It's because you're a mess that I recommend you *talk to a lawyer*. To start, at least a little, some process for sorting out your thoughts, examining your options, getting *out* of the mess.

Even if you haven't made up your mind to break up, talk to a lawyer. The first meeting's often free. Just ask. No lawyer will allow a free initial consultation to go on for hours, but they'll give a solid 30 or 60 minutes, focused on you. And if you honestly describe your situation then ask them to speculate a little, they'll caveat a few million times but they will spitball how things might play out, the process, outcome and fees.

If that feels daunting, get help. Invite a trusted pal to be your wingman, to bolster you. To come to lawyer's offices, if you want. (Though, to preserve confidentiality, you may want to have your wingman wait in the lawyer's waiting room.) It's your call. And remember: Lawyers are humans. Serious, expert professionals, but always, humans. Not some alien race or mutant species, *sharkus-homo-sapiens*. Visualize your lawyer as your hair stylist. A hair stylist is an important advisor and employee—entrusted with your very *self*, your image and confidence, your personal brand. Do you choose a hair stylist carefully? Totally. Do you ask their advice? Constantly. Do you follow it? Usually, but not always. Do you let them have final say? Of course not. You're in charge of you.

One last thing:

It's OK to change lawyers.

I've worked with many lawyers, in many situations. Not all were brilliant, effective or even honest. Yes, I, self-proclaimed Mr. Expert, lecturing you, screwed up royally, several times. Alas, I too am human. But when I realized I had the wrong lawyer, I fired them. If you screw up, fire yours. There's no need for some melodramatic scene. A simple, polite email will do.

Lawyers come in all colors, shapes, sizes, intelligences and capabilities. They have brilliant days and awful ones. *Talk to more than one.* Until you find one you just plain feel good about and feel comfortable talking to. As a person. Check references, of course. But if you don't feel good about a lawyer, move on. Don't work with someone you don't like. The world is full of lawyers.

Still, most lawyers I've worked with have been great. Saved my butt. Helped make me successful. And happy. How? By being lawyers. That is, by being knowledgeable and comfortable with the law and how the system works. By giving me honest advice even when I wasn't listening well. By keeping costs fair.

It's so understandable people are wary of lawyers. Attorneys are highly educated, richly rewarded experts with all sorts of privileges and can be tough and arrogant. They know the system much better than most people and unethical ones can work that to their own advantage. But whatever. It's silly risky—and can be *tragic*—to enter a legal dispute without legal counsel.

A breakup is a transit to a new life, new opportunities, hopefully exciting new worlds and people. Extricating yourself from a serious relationship inevitably comes with tough challenges and often demanding legal issues. *F*** it, get a lawyer.* Starting anew is too precious and important to trust to amateurs... like *us*.

Exercise

Part 1

Do the *The BIG 3*—a quick model for a simple master plan to manage your attorney (and your breakup.) Change your mind anytime, but in broad terms decide where you want to end up, and how to get there.

And forget nuances or specifics. This is *BIG* picture time:

BIG 1: Generally, how should things be divided?

Do you want to divide everything—assets, debts, kids—roughly 50/50? If yes, say so and don't pretend otherwise—that's a waste of time, money and good will.

If not, ok, but then what? Your ex can have 100%—you just want to be done? Or your ex can have zero and you're ready for the fight? Or divide some things 50/50 but not others? And how many of those others are scuffle-worthy? And how far from 50/50 do you think's right?

Whatever your positions, do you have good reasons for them? Reasons a *Judge* will agree with, even if your ex doesn't?

BIG 2: What's the breakup budget?

How much can you and your ex together spend on your breakup? It's likely you'll split the cost roughly equally. (Sorry, get used to it.) *So setting emotions aside, how much can you two really afford and not regret it when the heat cools?*

The heat cools quickly, probably faster than you expect. So are you going to waste, er, I mean, spend money on score settling? Try not to let present emotions cause you to spend money you later may wish you still had. Is fighting worth an additional $2,000? $5,000? Do you want to spend $5,000 to maybe get $7,500? What's the emotional cost of the fight worth? If the argument is over something meaningful, maybe it is. But maybe not. Try to be honest with yourself.

In any case, are you at risk of being financially stressed when the breakup is done? Can you contain breakup costs now, so that doesn't happen? Do. Seriously, *do*. So few breakup fights feel worth it later, after time has passed.

BIG 3: What's the breakup schedule?

Is time a factor? Would a speedy breakup benefit you enough that you'd be willing to be less demanding?

Divorces can get done in a few months or a few years—at what point will you *so* want to be free of the stress that the fight seems counterproductive? How about now? Are you really OK if fighting drags things out?

And try to coordinate your breakup schedule with real life. Who moves out? When? When do you tell the kids? Are there any ticking clocks—any work, school, social or medical things—that may influence a breakup schedule?

Part 2

Lawyer up.

Take a step into attorney world—don't worry, it's free, no obligations.

Get personal referrals for divorce lawyers. There's no better way to find one. Then call a few—not just one—and ask for a free, initial consultation. Almost all will do this. It's standard.

Then go meet them.

You don't need to make any commitments. Plan to walk out of meetings saying, *Thank you for your time, I have a lot to think over, I'll be back in touch.*

If for any reason whatsoever you don't like an attorney, just scratch them from your list. Go with your gut - if it doesn't feel right, it's not. And feel free to end a meeting abruptly, if you want to. Be polite of course, but just say, *I'm sorry, its me not you but I'm not comfortable, I think I should be on my way.* Most attorneys will be a little surprised, maybe, but they'll be polite back and that will be that. And if an attorney responds harshly, congratulations, you made the right call!

If cost is an issue, say so. More than once if needed. Ask the lawyer to rough guess how much your divorce will cost. They may squirm, or say (truthfully) that costs vary widely. But then you say, *I understand that but I'd still really appreciate at least an estimated range. Say, no more than X but no less than Y.* If an attorney has been in business any time at all they know what a typical client ends up spending. So you can ask for that: *What does your typical client with a profile like me end up spending?* If a lawyer refuses to talk plainly about cost, easy peasey, politely depart. And go meet another.

This process is free but the education is priceless.

Money

Can't buy me love.
—The Beatles

Money may not be the root of all evil, but too often it is the root of why people stay in unhappy couples.

Don't stay in a bad relationship over money.

If you do, at least be honest: *Price your happiness.* If Satan offers you $1,000,000 a year for life, but only on the condition you're unhappy every single day, will you do it?

What price are you selling your happiness for now?

I know, no one can just ignore finances. We need to make decisions based on reality, not wishes. But in unhappy relationships, there's another reality to consider: You'll be dead one day. Soon, in the greater scheme of things. So maybe money shouldn't rule your biggest of big-pictures. Maybe you're at risk of being so distracted by such things that one day you'll look in a mirror and gasp: *I'm so old. Where did my life go?*

Will today's money anxiety feel paramount then?

‹‖›

Now you're thinking: Well, sure, but how does that help pay the rent?

Good question.

Actually it does help.

Then again, maybe you're not thinking "the rent" is the issue. Maybe you believe you have enough money, you just have no idea how it all works or how to manage things, so you're fearful being on your own won't be liberating, it'll be a crushing burden.

Fair enough. But my prescription is the same.

If money stress of *any* sort is holding you in an unhappy relationship, that's at least partially from feeling *powerless*— fearing finances are beyond your control. So for me, the remedy is apparent: Get some control. Manage money anxiety by understanding things, even just a little bit more.

Even the tiniest improvements go a long way. Don't try to be a professional, just slightly more money-comfortable. And yes, even you, normal human, can do it. Even if things are really rotten and complicated and aren't going to change soon. Even then, having money stuff start to feel even the smallest bit more manageable allows you to start to think about plans, some tiny, first steps aimed at improving the things that you now see a bit more clearly.

And taking those steps *does* help pay the rent. And does help find your confidence.

As the man said, *We have nothing to fear but fear itself.* Since I can't know you or your situation, I'm all about trying to help with money "fear itself." The goal isn't to comprehend things to where nothing surprising or unpleasant occurs—that's impossible. It's just to feel a bit more in charge of *ourselves*. To manage our anxiety not have it manage us. We're human, we know chaos is always at the door. But we can learn to tune out some of the noise, not panic when the hard stuff does happen.

How? By acquiring *knowledge*. Not once, but as a lifelong commitment to do the work to be modestly well informed. Even if you're genuinely struggling, when you get a half-decent grasp of your circumstances, anxiety will consume you less. That's just common sense, no?

Of course, this isn't some remedy for truly tough predicaments. *If you have real problems, even with buckets of knowledge you'll still have them.* But hopefully you'll own them, not the other way around. Enough that you'll embark on some kind of plan to improve things, and to cope, day by day, find some calm and structure in your money world, and some time for your *other* big issues...

Like whether or not to stay in a bad relationship.

⟨⟩

So, *what* knowledge can start moving us past "fear itself"?

Let's call it *The Worst Case Scenario*.

If as a result of your breakup, 100% of the shit hits 100% of the fans, what's life like? How bad is it? Can you even handle the thought? Can you imagine getting out of bed every day and saying, *F*** it, I'm still alive, so it's a good day?* Then just getting on with your new life? Or is *The Worst Case Scenario* so awful you'd rather stay unhappy, maybe forever?

To see, let's get comfortable with two big money concepts:

1) Income

Meaning, money coming in to your household. From work. Investments. Alimony or child support. Wherever. If you have decent income, it often doesn't matter what else goes down—for example, your breakup can't make you totally helpless, at least.

Imagine your relationship is really over. The deal's complete, everything's divided up, you're on your own. It's really all completely done. But you don't have *squat*. It really is *The Worst Case Scenario*. You have no money. No investments, no retirement accounts. No property to speak of—no home that's owned, no car you don't owe too much money on, no insurance policies to cash out, no jewelry to sell. Just a few suitcases of your personal stuff. Otherwise, zilch.

And you have liabilities. Rent, or car payments, or student loans, or taxes you owe. So you have less than nothing—you have debts. And if you have kids, they're with you much of the time. So parenting money needs are the same or worse.

UGH.

Better to stay in your unhappy relationship?

No, not if you have dependable, sufficient *income*. Money coming in regularly. Enough to pay bills, love your kids, live your life.

And remember, it's your *new* life. Even in this dreadful scenario, whatever relationship pain, sadness, resentment, brooding or anger was in your life, is past. And you have chunks of your life back—all the time you used to spend interacting with (or avoiding) your ex. You're free of that now, and when you look at the whole, big, big picture, you're just a regular joe or jane, one of millions of decent, loving people working their butts off to manage a single adult household.

So do you have income? After breaking up, will you? If yes, then even in *The Worst Case Scenario,* woohoo, you're not screwed. You're off to discover your new life.

But wait, not yet. You need a little deeper knowledge to really get a grip on your money stress. Make a *Simple Monthly Budget*—a list of what you guess it will cost you, post-breakup, to live every month—to pay debts (credit cards, student loans, etc.) plus whatever else you need (rent, gas, food, clothes, etc.) Then compare that to your (also guessed-at) post-breakup monthly income. If you show a *deficit* (a shortfall caused by having less monthly income than expenses) you need to make a plan to get more income and/or reduce expenses. So roll up your sleeves and take a whack at that. Even if belt-tightening is unpleasant, I predict you'll still feel good about having the knowledge and control to just... deal.

Of course, if your *Simple Monthly Budget* shows a *surplus* (you have extra money after paying monthly expenses,) congratulations, you get to decide what to do with that cash.

But no matter what, even in *The Worst Case Scenario,* you're on your way.

Does it feel good to know that? Or at least, a bit less stressful?

<H>

Wait. You *don't* have any income?

Ah.

Well, sorry, but... get a job.

First, same as above, make a *Simple Monthly Budget.* If your income is zero, the deficit will be large but it'll tell you how much income you need to get by, either from alimony or child support (if you're eligible) or from take-home (after taxes) pay from your job. As well as if you need to reduce expenses.

Then go get a job.

Alas, you may need to let go of dreams about lifestyle or careers. Short term, right now, just get a job. Any job. If in your current relationship you're not responsible for earning money, no problem, no shame, but acknowledge that feeling powerless and trapped is at least partially tied to that. *And that that can change.*

Of course, if you're committed to never working, forever relying on someone else for support, ok, f*** it, stay in the relationship.

Otherwise, get a job.

And get ready for a really good feeling—it's amazing how empowered and confident you'll feel *just getting a job.*

Any frigging job.

There's no such thing as dishonorable work. All of us are only a generation or two from being peasants. My peasant grandparents were courageous, inspiring entrepreneurial successes—penniless, they *walked* out of eastern Europe to get to the U.S., where they didn't know a soul, didn't speak English, had no way to go back. But eventually they had work, homes and families. New lives. Peasants? No, brave, visionary humans with pride, dignity and drive—while cleaning other people's floors and sewing their socks. They wanted to start new lives, so *f*** it*, they did.

Your forebearers were like that. And you have their fighter DNA. Use it. Whatever your problems may be, they'd probably just make your ancestors laugh.

2) Nest eggs

Do you have a Nest Egg? You, personally. Any cash or possessions, beyond what you need to pay the bills every month. Not as a couple, as an individual. *The post-breakup you.*

Let's try figuring it out. First, guess, roughly-speaking, how much money and possessions you as a couple have, today. Wild guesses are fine.

Next, try to guess how much of it is likely to end up yours.

To do that, just pick some ratio you think will work. When a couple has *assets*—money, possessions, real estate or other property—in a breakup that all gets divided. Maybe the ratio is 50/50. Or 60/40. Or 90/10. Some ratio or another will be agreed on. (Or else couples can use some item-by-item plan, where they decide what belongs to just one of them and what to both. Then somehow how to divide what belongs to both. For now, just use a rough ratio.)

Of course, debts will be divided as well. Mortgages, car loans, credit card debts, student loans, etc.

These type of negotiations can be easy. Or war. Here, it doesn't matter. Just make your best guess as to what all of your and your partner's money and possessions are worth, including your house if you own one. Don't include literally everything, just whatever is valuable enough that someday it could be sold, if necessary. For example, *don't* try to value pots and pans. But jewelry, yes.

Again, don't sweat this, just roughly estimate. Then, try to roughly add up your debts. Is there a mortgage? About how much credit card debt do you both have?

Then apply whatever ratio you decided on to both assets and debts. And take a minute to decide: Will *everything* get split using your ratio or are there significant exceptions? Say, a sports car that will definitely go with you, along with its big car loan. If so, add that into your column accordingly, and if that tips the balance of the ratio you decided on, move something to your ex's column so the final totals come out to your ratio.

In any case, remember, don't worry about accuracy, guesstimates are fine, just scratch out quick numbers: Total assets. Total debts. How split the assets? How split the debts?

Got those rough numbers? Now subtract *your share* of the post-breakup debts from *your share* of the post-breakup assets. Good work, that's your post-breakup *Nest Egg*.

If it's zero, so be it. Welcome to Club Normal, that'll be true for many people. Few folks have material Nest Eggs, whether married, divorced or single. (But it's never too late to start accumulating one.)

In any case, go back to your *Simple Monthly Budget*. If the *Budget* shows a surplus, congrats, that surplus *adds* to your Nest Egg every month. If it shows a deficit, that reduces your Nest Egg each month. Get it?

There are no right or wrong answers to these things, only knowledge. The point is to learn to be comfortable with the issues, and with revisiting and revising your rough numbers from time to time. With that, you get decent control over your overall situation—and, ergo, you reduce money stress.

Knowledge *is* power, baby.

<hr />

Feel better at all? Even just a smidgen?

Of course, post-breakup, your financial situation may be quite different than what came before. You may have to change your life in meaningful ways. But... isn't that precisely *why* we break up unhappy relationships? Changing one's life is the *prize*, as well as the price.

It's true, if you have to consider downsizing your lifestyle you may long for impulse shopping or eating out more. But with the ability to visualize ahead of time what that life may be like, do you feel at least a little more calm and empowered? And more importantly, do you still feel you can't leave your bad relationship?

I don't know you of course, but I predict that, if you do leave, and start a new life, you won't wish you'd stayed in such an unhappy, unloved place, just for money.

Anyway, that's my $0.02.

(*Sorry, couldn't resist.*)

↔

One last thing:

Be smart and tough but avoid nickel and diming.

And its corollary:

Try to show no anger over your ex's nickel and diming.

When you decide to move on, dividing up money *perfectly* shouldn't be a priority. Don't squabble over every dime. You'll be glad. You'll be free sooner, and feeling proud of yourself. Yes, be firm on the things that matter. But not for the last buck or word.

Try it. Next time your partner is haggling over a dollar here or there, just say, no big deal, you take it. You'll feel great about your maturity, and "eyes on the prize" strength to let it go in order *to go*. And you may get the satisfaction of seeing your partner realize they're silly and small. If in the final accounting, the dimes add up to some decent sum, making the breakup math slightly in your ex's favor, take the long view. Meaning, who cares. That's the cost of *a new life*. And trust me, a year from then—maybe just months from then—odds are, you'll barely remember what that squabble was even about.

On the other hand, if you just enjoy arguing over a few bucks—or if you care so much about money and material things that you'll stay forever in a rotten relationship—you do have a good chance for that ultimate achievement:

Exercise

You just heard me extol the virtues of making a *Simple Monthly Budget*. And you should. But here, let's expand the idea, get you an even higher level of money knowledge and control: Make a *Simple Life Budget*.

(If this makes you groan a little, welcome to Club Normal Human Being. But you'll almost certainly have to do this someday, so why not take a first crack at it now? I predict: You'll thank me.)

Here are the basic assumptions you'll use. (This is just for now. You can change assumptions later any way you wish.)

1. You broke up. You're now on your own.
2. Everything got split 50/50.
3. No one pays, or gets, alimony or child support.

Here are the basic numbers to hash out:

N—Nest Egg

N is the rough total value of all your cash, property and possessions. That is, roughly 50% of whatever you had as a couple. (Remember, the basic assumption is a 50/50 split.) Yes, N can be zero.

L—Liabilities

L is the total of all debts, bills and costs (e.g. groceries, gasoline, etc.) that *must* be paid by you, now, as a post-breakup single adult household, every month. (Remember, the assumption for now is, no one pays alimony or child support.)

These imagined monthly costs should be similar to what you really do pay now, as a two-adult household. In many ways, a household is a household—utilities, insurances, cleaning, etc. But if you simply don't know, guess. For example, you may not know if you'll rent or own your residence after you break up. So just guess some monthly payment number that will either be a mortgage payment or rent.

I—Income

I is the total of every dime from every source that comes in each month. Pay from work, investments, whatever. (Remember, the assumption is no one gets alimony or child support.) Yes, it can be zero.

D—Discretionary Income

D is whatever money you have left over from your monthly Income *after* you've paid your monthly Liabilities. So calculate D using this formula: **D=I minus L.**

Yes, D may be a negative number.

T—Time to Nest-Egg-Zero

If D is a negative number—if your monthly Liabilities are greater than your monthly Income—then **T** is the amount of Time (in months) before your Nest Egg runs out. (If your Nest Egg is zero to start with, see below.)

Meaning, presumably you dip into your Nest Egg each month to keep paying monthly Liabilities, while you figure out how to either increase your Income or reduce Liabilities.

The formula is: **T=N divided by D.**

Note: To use the formula, make D a positive number. Say D equals -$5,000 (negative $5,000 per month) and N equals $50,000. To use the formula make D positive: $50,000 divided by $5,000, not -$5,000. That way T is a positive number, too. In this case, 10, meaning, 10 months of T, time, before N, Nest Egg, is zero. That is: If you have $5,000 more Liabilities than Income each month but have a $50,000 Nest Egg, you can pay Liabilities for 10 months before your Nest Egg runs out.

If your Nest Egg *starts* as zero, then T is zero—you have zero months to figure out how to keep going. You're in default on your obligations now. You have to increase Income or reduce Liabilities immediately. Some people solve this with credit cards, borrowing more and more, enjoying the usually low minimum monthly payments required. But over time, this is often a dangerous fool's game, basically praying for a miracle, postponing yet worsening the day of reckoning. If you have to borrow, borrow. But if you don't *have* to borrow from a huge faceless corporation that views you as a number, try not to. If we borrow from friends or family, it can be awkward and embarrassing but at least we know we're not risking getting chewed up and spit out by a merciless machine.

⟷

As you play with these numbers and gain a little knowledge, go back and change the core assumptions then run numbers again. For example, try making a more realistic estimate about whether your split will be 50/50 or something else. Or whether anyone will get alimony and child support, and how much for how long...

Extra Credit

Make a *Personal Statement of Net Worth*—a more detailed description of your Nest Egg. It's a healthy, useful knowledge and control building exercise to create this, then periodically revisit and update it as life unfolds.

First, list roughly what your wealth and possessions are worth:

- Cash
- Your primary home (if you own it. 50% if you co-own it.)

- Your investments: Mutual funds, stocks, bonds, your 401(k), your IRA, real estate other than your primary residence.
- Sell-able possessions: Cars, boats, recreational vehicles, motor homes, second homes, jewelry, art, etc. (Don't bother with TVs, furniture and appliances—such things can be personally valuable but are not really financially valuable.)
- Inheritances you know will come to you someday.
- Cash values of life insurance policies. (Some policies have cash values, some do not.)
- Ownership interests in businesses that one day could get sold. (Be honest—your coaching practice may be a terrific business but likely nobody's ever going to buy it.)
- Legal judgements you are owed. (For example, if you won a lawsuit but haven't received the settlement yet.)
- Tax refunds you know you are owed.

Total it all up. That number is your Gross Net Worth, or **GNW.**

Now list all your liabilities and debts. Not the normal monthly operating costs, like utility bills. Your lumpy, longer term debts. Use the total amounts owed, not monthly payments owed. (That is, use the sum total of *all* the monthly payments still owed):

- Mortgages.
- Home equity loans.
- Car loans or leases.
- Credit card balances.
- Personal loans or lines of credit.
- Tax liens or balances owed to the government.
- Legal judgements you must pay.

Total all that up. That's your Gross Liabilities, or **GL.**

Now we can state your Personal Net Worth, or **PNW**:

PNW=GNW minus GL

It's just a number. There's no right or wrong one. But it's good to have a rough idea—when you break up it could matter. For example, if it's a *longterm marriage* (more than 7 years—for more on this see *Divorce Dictionary*) the couple's PNW—*their combined assets and liabilities*—will probably get divided 50/50.

But if a couple's combined PNW is negative—if their liabilities exceed their assets—there may be thorny issues to work out.

Of course, PNW doesn't take into account *income*—wages, salary, investment income, alimony, etc—and if you have enough income to make debt payments, and pay off debts fully over time, you're ok. (And a member of Club Normal, a common human.)

On the other hand, if you have a negative PNW and your income is *not* enough to make the situation work, and you can't imagine ever fully paying off debts, you probably should have a free, initial consultation with a bankruptcy attorney. It's a challenging situation, but we abolished debtors prisons in the USA centuries ago, so there are usually reasonable solutions.

Heart

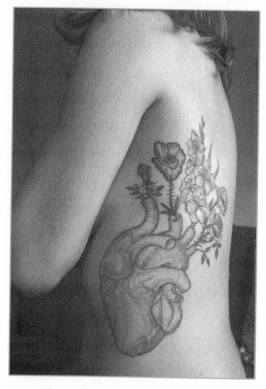

I haven't found out yet:
Is this as grown-up as we ever get?
Maybe this is as good as it gets.
And years may go by,
But I think the heart remains a child.
The mind may grow wise,
But the heart just sulks and it whines and
remains a child.
> —Everything But The Girl
> *The Heart Remains A Child*

Tradition

Our old ways were once new, weren't they?
—Tevye, *Fiddler on the Roof*

*Would you believe in what you believe in if you
were the only one who believed it?*
—Kanye West

If you bow to the institution of marriage as a revered tradition, a bond to the past and root of human morality, good news: You can get up off your knees. Matrimony is ancient but it offers continuity to hardly anything. The concept changes, constantly.

Don't stay in an unhappy relationship out of respect for tradition. Your future matters much more than history.

Cultural norms come and go but you're struck with *you*. For life. Tradition isn't a roadmap to proven morality, it's like a whiteboard covered in post-it notes. Over time, whatever sticks, sticks. And some post-its get pressed back on. We can and do find in history and tradition whatever we happen to want to

83

justify. If you need a moral compass, don't look back, look *in*— inside you.

No, this isn't an argument for moral relativism. I don't believe all human beliefs and practices are equally valid. Not even close. Slavery has played a huge role in human history. I unreservedly condemn it. Likewise, I don't trash the past just because it is the past. The concept of a sabbath, a regular break from work with time for family and spirituality, is ancient. I unreservedly endorse it.

But my point remains: What we view as norms are mostly just recent and ephemeral trends. Here today, gone tomorrow. And given how long *your* life hopefully will be, consider: By the time you're on your deathbed you won't regret following your heart today because by then, your thoughts and beliefs about so many behaviors will have changed, many times.

I don't make that prediction because I claim to know you. I don't. And I can't. Well, other than that you're a *human*. And human cultures, practices and morals change over time. Often, radically. Here are some historical examples:

Today we view marriage as a romantic life experience, and falling in love as a precondition for serious longterm relationships. But for almost all of human history, marriage had little if anything to do with romance. In his scholarly book, *Kinship and Marriage,* Rutgers University anthropologist Robin Fox estimates that the vast majority of marriages throughout history have been between first or second cousins—practical unions created to maintain family continuity and property. Today in many parts of the world many marriages are still between cousins.

The whole notion of fidelity or cheating, of people taking oaths to only have physical relationships with their one, pledged partner, isn't a consistent or uniform idea. Monogamy isn't even common in human history, it's only a relatively recent norm. In most of the past, polygamy was common, not controversial, albeit practiced mostly by wealthy and aristocratic men, with multiple wives. That's way out of favor in the Western world today, of course, but many of our heroes from religion and scripture were polygamists, like King David, King Solomon and the Prophet Mohammed. And polygamy was a global practice, not just Western. It's still practiced in many places in the Islamic world and Africa. Hindu nobility practiced polygamy for eons. The Buddha was born into a polygamist family. Monogamy as we think of it now only became a norm around the 9th century A.D. when the Catholic Church won over European nobility. Before mixing with Europeans, many Native American and indigenous peoples were polyamorous, with men and women alike bonding with multiple partners.

So why do so many of us still act in such judge-or-be-judged ways, as if there were clear rules for human behavior?

It's not our fault. It's history's. DNA doesn't care what we do as long as we reproduce, but 10,000 years of civilization burned in our sub-consciousness does. Or did. Or maybe still does—we're not really sure. We modern people wrestle with that every day. Is XYZ a sin? Or is it a cherished part of the human tapestry? Or who even cares? That uncertainty can be agonizing for people, causing shame, fear and anger. And of course, it's a heavy factor in why people default to staying in unhappy relationships. Doing that hurts but feels safer for traditionally, unhappiness is the norm.

Consider the historical tidbits I just shared, about cousins, polygamy and things. Do we think all those people were happily married? Emotionally content by our our standards? Not a chance. Their unions were practical affairs at best. It's true they didn't marry for romance so their expectations were different, but they were still human, still pined for love. So in all likelihood, they were lonely and frustrated. But who had time for love? There were so many other priorities: Food, clothing and shelter. Money. Labor—it took several adults plus a brood of kids to operate a farm. Or a store or workshop. Marriage was a business deal and if everyone had a roof, clothing and food, congratulations, you won the game of survival.

But us, we do have time. And opportunity. Just consider how biologically and mathematically *different* our lives are versus previous generations. When Social Security was created in the US in 1935, the age at which people could start receiving benefits (Social Security checks) was set at 62. Why? Because in 1935, that was the average life expectancy for a man. But today life expectancies are in the mid 80s or longer. We live 15-25 years longer today than just two or three generations ago.

Likewise, our health, our very biologies, are different—we have wonderfully raised expectations of not only how long we'll live but how active we can be and for how long, and what medical conditions are nuisances not traumas, what chronic afflictions are manageable not fatal, plus all sorts of modern tools to stay active—antibiotics, Spanx, hip replacements, supplements, yoga, orthopedic shoes, viagra, stents, pain relievers, plastic surgery, botox, Match.com. There's simply no comparison of today versus yesteryears of what's to be expected when two people say "til death do us part."

In the past, our modern expectations about emotional and spiritual rewards, and how long life actually would be, were not on marrying people's minds. Instead there was a much more simple calculation: Hopefully you at least liked—or didn't hate—your spouse. Sometimes you barely knew them. Or other people decided who married who. But if your spouse wasn't too horrible, maybe eventually you'd grow to like them, maybe even love them, in some way. If not, well, you'd just be like everybody else you knew, plus all the generations that went before.

Of course in the old days people were still people. Still fragile, vulnerable humans, who sought solace and love. They just didn't expect *marriage* to provide it. Stability, yes, hopefully. But emotional fulfillment, unlikely. Which is why Hollywood movies were so instantly popular in the early days of cinema—they offered dreams of romance to a public starved of it, an audience who felt like Dorothy in *The Wizard of Oz*, longing for joy, a thing so unlikely it existed, say, only over the rainbow.

Lucky us, we live here and now. Maybe we can't escape history and old morals but we don't have to be bound by them. Today, we do seek love and romance, we're obsessed by the search for love and romance because we can be, and because *of course we do*—life is so much more rewarding with loving relationships. And we have the time and opportunity to try to find them.

So today divorce is common and growing more so, because life is long but time is short, and we're free to look for precious ultimate rewards like love—but only if we're free, that is. Such rewards are painfully difficult to find in any event, let alone if we are restricted to one partner for life. So if tradition and history are impediments, well, then to hell with tradition and history. Staying in an unhappy relationship—abandoning the quest for love, forever—is, for many of us, just not an option. We want to keep looking. Why pay attention to cultural antecedents that preach to stop, just because we didn't get it right the first time?

In the contemporary world, we can be free of shame if we choose to be, and of making decisions based on what others think, now or in the past. All fifty US states and the District of Columbia have mercifully even codified that into law: Divorces are granted as "no fault", literally meaning, no one is at fault, nobody's to blame, culpability and guilt aren't factors because a marriage ending is just such a common, obvious thing. Such tradition-free laws are in place in many other countries as well, including Australia, Canada, China, Mexico, Russia, Spain and Sweden. And the "no fault" movement is spreading rapidly.

Today, some folks even celebrate their disunion. Some splitting couples hold divorce parties, not unlike wedding parties, to announce their breakup and demonstrate that it's all ok, in fact it's better than ok, it's a happy life event. The two former partners are still friends, wish each other well, and want all their peeps to help them commemorate their time of union and the—yes—cheerful occasion of their separation.

What a great new, er, *tradition*.

Of course some people are still harsh and judgemental and always will be. But in today's world, we can choose: Let them control us. Or else, control ourselves, and say:

F*** tradition. I'm getting a divorce.

Exercise

Step in my Time Machine to revisit your history and see the future. I've invited some very special guests to assist you, three super wise people with something in common—*they're all you*:

1. *EarlyYou*: You, just before you married or committed.
2. *NowYou*: You, right now.
3. *FutureYou*: You, 25 years from now.

All three *You*'s: Reflect on the saying, *If I only knew then what I know now*. *NowYou* tell *EarlyYou*: What's necessary to know about longterm relationships in general? About their own one and partner? About themself? About what happiness is and how to seek it? Likewise, what can *FutureYou* teach *NowYou*?

Use specifics. What did *EarlyYou* feel about, say, "snuggling"? How does *NowYou* feel about it now? 25 years from now, how does *FutureYou* feel? Did *FutureYou* fix any "snuggling" issues that bothered *NowYou*? Use any topics, but here are suggestions:

- Snuggling. Hand holding. Non-sex physical affection. Important? Frequency matter? Freedom to be naughty?
- Sex.
- Monogamy and fidelity.
- Intellectual and values compatibility.

- Day in and day out conversation.
- Humor. Important to find one's partner to be funny?
- Household cleanliness and clutter.
- The value (or horror) of fighting and arguing.
- Boredom. How much is ok? How much is too much?
- Homebodiness. Is going out important? How often?
- Friends. What qualities make friends really friends? Do both partners agree? And like each other's friends?
- Moodiness and negativity. How much is normal? Where's the line between sympathy and indulgence?
- Time together. How much is too little? Too much?
- Health and fitness. Is there such a thing as too much?
- Style, grooming and personal appearance. Is slovenliness ok? Is fanatic attention to one's own appearance ok?
- Money and material things.
- Careers. Yours and your partners. Too much focus? Not enough? Is big ambition a positive trait? Or a negative?

All three *You*'s should *individually* give each item a score:

-1 — Yuck. Painful subject, a negative in my life.

0 — Zero. Not important, don't care.

1 — Meh. Can't ignore it, but wish I could.

2 — Ok. Deserving of my time and energy but not much.

3 — Good. An important priority. But negotiable when needs be.

4 — Critical. Essential to my life and happiness. Not negotiable.

How do scores change over time? Did *EarlyYou* give "snuggling" a 2 but *NowYou* and *FutureYou* give it a 4? Etc. Also, does the overall pattern of scores changing over time reveal anything about you? How you are evolving as you age? Finally, what if anything does that pattern of change reveal about how you feel about your current relationship? Is it enabling or blocking the path leading to *FutureYou*? And how will *Future You* feel about your current status, looking back from 25 years hence?

Don't take the bait

Don't wanna fight no more.
I don't wanna fight no more.
—Alabama Shakes

To smile.
> —Dwight D. Eisenhower, when
> asked "What was your most
> important job in World War II?"

One reason people stay in unhappy relationships is so common, so obvious, it's not often discussed:

Conflict avoidance. Plain old conflict avoidance.

So many of us just don't want to deal with strife. To where we don't do things we should—like trying to either fix or end an unhappy relationship. Instead, we let things fester, as we suffer, usually in silence, for years.

I'm not condemning this. I'm guilty of it. And as I said, I think it's incredibly common. In fact, I think the only folks who *don't*

routinely avoid conflict tend to have been trained for that—
attorneys, diplomats, therapists, business dealmakers.

So if this factors in your thoughts about your relationship, maybe
we can train *you*.

<⏸️>

I think avoiding conflict is one of our species' evolutionary
default settings: Fight or flight? *Flight!*

Why? Well, here's an obvious reason: Most of us are decent,
good-hearted people. Another of our default settings is, we want
to help others, or at least, not hurt anyone. So openly engaging in
conflict feels like a violation of that core value.

Even more basic, we don't want to hurt *us*. We're fragile, every
single one of us. We need to protect ourselves. And if we're in an
unhappy relationship, we feel trapped and especially weak. So we
stay put, and silent.

But I believe we can break that cycle. And confidently—but
gently—deal with conflict, without hurting anyone, or ourselves.
And become liberated to try to live whatever life we wish.

How?

Don't take the bait.

<⏸️>

What's "bait"? Sometimes a person will try to get what they want
by "baiting" another, tempting them into letting down their
guard, into being emotional not rational, feeling combative not
calm—and so, open themselves to control and manipulation by
engaging willy-nilly in conflict. They usually do this by some
slight or provocation, whether big and blatant or small and
subtle, either by aggressive action (that is, by doing something)
or by being passive aggressive (by *not* doing something.)

That's bait. Don't take it.

It doesn't matter what your partner, or anyone, says or does. Rise above. Stay calm. Turn the other cheek. Then turn it again. Don't react, respond. And forgive the unforgivable. *Especially the unforgivable.*

Look open conflict square in the eye... and shrug. *No matter what it takes or how long, your first response to conflict should be... no response at all.*

The point isn't to ignore conflict, it's to ignore the temptation to get agitated. Control conflict with cool. Keep eyes on the prize— the freedom to have a new life—and meet conflict with calm, a steady indifference. Even if that indifference is completely phony and you're just pretending. *Especially then.*

There's a big side benefit to this approach: *It's an effective strategy to win disputes.* If you don't take the bait, you buy time to become more wise, a better negotiator. To focus on substance, not emotion.

If bait's dangled, close your eyes and concentrate on slowing your heart rate. On steadying your breathing. Take as much time as you need. There's no rush. When you regain calm, then you can decide *if* or *how* to respond.

In other words, using whatever method works best for you, by patiently allowing yourself to move past any initial waves of emotion, you become empowered and wise.

I mean, right? Can anyone better deal with tough challenges when overcome by emotion?

⟷

I know. This strategy sounds obvious, pedestrian. And it is. *Yet this may be the most difficult thing we do in life.* We're emotional beings: Turning down or turning off emotions isn't natural. And when things really push our buttons, it's *soooo* hard. But when liberating ourselves from unhappy relationships, we need to put on our Spock ears, turn down our emotional radar, and stay calm and focused on the big goal: moving on.

Remember: *Once you've decided to breakup, the big, main conflict is over.* Settled. Done. Yes, there are all sorts of complex issues to be worked out over time. Maybe you haven't even gotten through the scary act of telling your partner it's over. But in the big, big, big picture, the details and challenging situations of doing the breakup are all just mile markers on the map, not the destination. *You're moving on, to a new life.* The core, huge conflict was the stay-or-go decision—and congratulations, you did that. Now it's time to deal with all the implications of that decision, and get to it's penultimate resolution: Your new life.

So don't take the bait.

This doesn't mean cave in, or abandon needs or demands. It's a "don't bellow, be mellow" strategy, yes, but if you like, use it as a way to stick to your guns and get what you want—most crucially, by removing the conflict avoidance anxiety that gets in the way of tackling things crisply and head on. Don't overlook the *power* of being calm. By not taking the bait you can *win* disputes, as your risen-above-it attitude makes your ex (or whoever) feel silly for indulging in immature, manipulative melodramas that just waste time. (And who knows? Feeling foolish, maybe your ex will abandon baiting and just focus on getting the deal done.)

So don't get mad, get free.

When we take the bait, we reduce ourselves to an unthinking state, with a reflexive, childlike brain flooded with adrenaline, reacting, not responding, often in self-destructive ways. *But that's not inevitable.* That's a choice we make...or don't.

Here's an example:

Early in their breakup, a close friend and his then-wife decided that he'd be the one to move out. She'd keep their house. It wasn't hard. She felt strongly about the house. He didn't.

But she wanted him to move out immediately and he disagreed. They were in complicated negotiations about where their teenage daughters would live, and when. Not an unusual difference perhaps, but not one getting resolved quickly. So he wouldn't move out until that was resolved. For one thing, he didn't want their kids (or anyone) to think he'd depart without having a complete answer to the kids' inevitable question: *Where are we all living?* For another, he thought continuing to live together would create healthy pressure to not let that negotiation drag on. And their house was big enough for each of them to have their own, equally nice bedrooms and bathrooms—in fact, they'd already been living in separate rooms for a while.

His soon-to-be-ex disagreed. She felt their daughters were mature, knew their parents were divorcing and could handle ambiguity for a while. And that it was more important for she and him to really separate, start clearing the air and settling down for real, and that they could more easily complete negotiations without awkward cohabitation.

But he stood firm and wouldn't leave. She couldn't order him out, they weren't divorced yet, it was still his house, too. For a while it was tough. But then in a few months they worked out a parenting plan, where their daughters would live, and when. And so, while they still had other substantive issues to resolve, he moved out.

Immediately, she changed the locks on the house.

And when she gave new keys to the daughters she said it was because she was afraid their father would be in the house when he wasn't supposed to be.

For him, that was *intense* bait.

He was livid. WTF! There was no history of him ever doing anything even remotely like being in her (or anyone's) space against their wishes or being threatening in any way. No such allegations were being made in their divorce. And when he moved out, he was completely out. Their stuff had been amicably divided and his was all at his new place. So he had no reason to even want to be at that house, other than to pick up or drop off the kids.

Maybe his soon-to-be-ex was so consumed by the *conflict* aspect of their breakup (as opposed to its *liberation* side) that she just wanted to prod him with a spear. Even if that meant painting him as some kind of brute, or scaring their daughters. Or maybe it was a deliberate provocation, *because of* such things. After all, if he took the bait—overreacted, went a little nuts—he'd prove the thesis. If he got enraged maybe he *was* irrational and scary. They still had issues to settle. And maybe she wanted to renegotiate the parenting schedule. What might a Judge do if he seemed threatening?

But he couldn't know her motives. So it was important he not take *that* bait, either—not become obsessed guessing what she was thinking. No, somehow he just had to be chill and let the big, big, big picture rule: Would feuding get him free faster? Or better? And when calm, he could admit the truth: She had every right to change the locks. It was her house now. And while he'll insist to his dying breath she had no reason to be afraid, he had to acknowledge that in breakups people feel vulnerable and if it made her feel better to change locks, she should. And yes, maybe she impugned him but whatever—he couldn't stop her.

So when he was calm it was clear:

Taking the bait would reward her, and hurt him.

More importantly, the real takeaway from her baiting him was, the sooner they were both free, the better.

I'd like to tell you he somehow just figured all this out on his own, he was some kind of wonderful inspired human, but no, he readily admits, he was just lucky: He had friends and family who gave sage advice—Breathe. Don't rush. Eyes on the big picture.

Can I be that friend for you?

Don't take the bait.

He didn't. He didn't react at all. For a while, when he picked up the kids, it was tense. She made him wait, insisted he stay outside, even in the snow. The daughters would sneak quizzical looks at him in such moments. But he didn't take *that* bait either—the temptation to badmouth her. He just kept breathing, made small talk and smiled, best he could. And when eventually the kids did broach the topic, he just smiled and said, *Well your mom and I aren't married anymore. It's her house. She can change the locks anytime she wants. She can paint the house with polka dots. It's her house.*

And that was a *big win* for him—it was instantly obvious from his daughters' faces they were delighted he didn't take the bait. He didn't get hot, didn't fight with their mom, didn't drag them into the middle.

But the *best* win was how good the whole episode made him feel. In the divorce, but more than that. As a person. He wasn't petty. He was calm, despite that inside he was raw.

Try it.

Want to avoid conflict? Don't take the bait. Life is full of disagreements and disputes. Save meltdowns for the truly few times (if ever) there's no other way. Instead, stay calm. Breathe. Engage if it's useful. Don't, if it isn't. Don't become obsessed with what, looking back someday, will be short term distractions. Keep your inner nav system programmed for the destination: your new life.

No matter how legitimate, emotional intensity fades. Even if your breakup is a hot mess. Eventually your new life will begin. You'll stop feeling, or even thinking about, past wrongs. I know, it's hard to imagine, but—*This too shall pass.*

Don't take the bait.

Exercise

Part 1: Juicy Bait

Try to imagine some situations where you may be vulnerable to juicy bait dangled in front of you.

And other scenes where you may be tempted to chum the waters with bait, hoping to ensnare your soon-to-be-ex.

Here's a common, bait-risky scenario:

Who gets the house? (Or the apartment or condo.)

"Who gets the house" is always a sticky, bait-rich dilemma, even in cases (such as my own) where the answer was quick and non-controversial. (She wanted the house, I was fine with that, we had the finances for her to get it without money acrobatics.)

The point is, "who gets the house" is an enormously important, deep, wildly disruptive situation in more or less all break ups—so the risk/temptation of chummed waters is huge.

Consider all the issues that need to get resolved and the resentments that may ensue: What if you have to leave and your ex gets to stay? What if you can't leave but your ex *can* so you're stuck there?

Bottom line, do you want the house? Really *really* want it?

So much you'll fight for it, and/or make sacrifices—very real financial sacrifices—to keep it? If it's a rental, odds are its relatively simple for one of you to walk away (though whoever stays behind has to agree to take on the lease all by themselves.) But maybe it's not so easy. Change may make a landlord nervous. One earner taking on the lease, not two. Or the person staying behind now searching for a roommate—and who gets to reference check this new roommate? Etc.

If you own a residence, things may get complicated quickly. Is there debt, a mortgage on the house? Are both of your names on both the house and the mortgage? How much is the house worth? Hopefully it's worth more than the mortgage—that amount (how much the house is worth beyond the amount of the mortgage) is called the "equity" in the house. Whoever leaves is entitled to half the "equity." How will that be paid? When will that be paid? Does the person staying behind have enough cash to even pay out half the "equity"? Will the lender (the bank or other financial institution that holds the mortgage) allow one of you to take on the entire debt? Does the person staying behind have good enough credit to sign up for that much debt?

Etc....

Then again, what if the reality is, nobody gets the house? It's just too expensive for either one of you to stay. It has to be sold. So even if you have the most loving and amicable break up in history, emotionally are you ok acknowledging you will never, ever get to go back there?

Nope. Just one day: Poof. It's gone. Somebody else's home now.

Do you care? Maybe that makes you giddy with joy. Maybe this is the best news you've had in years. Too many weird memories. Or you can't stand the place. Never could. You just went along to get along. Or maybe you used to think that place was *so you* but now you feel like it's so *not. Not the you you are today.*

Or maybe it's just a yawn. Who cares one iota for that house? It barely registers in your heart. Your ex can have it. Or not. Sell it. Whatever. It exerts no pull on you at all.

Isn't it best to evaluate those feelings in advance?

If nothing else, such prior evaluation prepares you for what, in most break ups, is a signature traumatic event.

As always, in this exercise you are not required to place your hand on a Bible and swear to whatever you're feeling today.

But do be honest and realistic. You and your partner have finally agreed to break up, now the "who gets the house" moment of truth is upon you, and your position is... what?

And also, for the sake of the exercise, imagine the worst. Even if your gut instinct is "who gets the house" isn't going to to be a big problem in your breakup. Still, imagine you and your soon-to-be-ex have a fundamental disagreement over the issue. Say, about the economics of one of you leaving and one staying.

Say your partner gets to stay. You have to leave. Before you know how much compensation if any you'll get from your ex for being the one to leave.

For example, if you're going to rent a place, do you have the cash for the three months rent that will be needed up front? Or a down payment on buying a place? If you're renting now, do you have a bunch of cash tied up in the down payment on the rental you now are leaving? Etc.

Ok, to resolve that short term, you're going to move in with some friends for a month or two. Just to defuse the tension in your breakup and have time to sort out the details.

And because you have a clear head, you're doing the "Pruning" exercise, figuring out what possessions go with you and what stay behind. You feel worried and a little pissed you're going to have to leave without a final financial deal in place and you want to at least be clear about the "pruning" of the stuff.

Out of nowhere, your soon-to-be-ex claims a deep attachment to some possession you know hasn't been important to them before.

But which *has* been important to *you* every day. Say, the expensive juicer you use to make your breakfast, always.

It's pretty clear you're being deliberately manipulated, to provoke you for some reason. Maybe just for the sheer fun and sport of seeing you melt down. Maybe to legitimately hurt you—that juicer cost $800. Maybe for some more abstract reason—your soon-to-be-ex is betting that if you freak out and melt down you'll be a much less effective negotiator and it'll be easier to get a better deal from you. Maybe there's deep rage here—seriously corrosive destructive anger—and maybe you do have a hot temper, and what's sought is for you to have a total meltdown, allowing your soon-to-be-ex to claim to be feared for their safety and call the police and have you arrested for domestic violence?

So... do you take the bait?

No. If you have any ability at all to remain calm and sane, do.

This doesn't mean you are forgiving your soon-to-be-ex's bad behavior. Or enabling it. Or anything of the sort.

You're doing a huge wonderful loving thing...

... for yourself.

I know, this can require a person to somehow channel the Mother Teresa and Mahatma Ghandi inside them. To be superhuman in instant awareness and forgiveness.

But the rewards are great. You will feel so... content. Mature. Liberated. Validated. Empowered.

Part 2: Go fish

Try to imagine some *real* bait-laden situations that may come up when you disentangle from your relationship or marriage. Imagine the worst... and visualize yourself having the temerity, control, vision and calm to not take the bait.

Be honest—also imagine situations where you're the one laying out the bait. You're the one who swears to only be respectful and amicable in public... but then deliberately tells someone close to your ex, a predictable gossip conduit, that your ex was a disappointment in bed.

I mean, what the hell, maybe that's true, maybe that's false, but you're feeling wounded by your soon-to-be-ex, they're behaving so coldly, so greedy, so hurtful, so narcissistic, so so so so...

So you're entitled to fight back. So you're just returning fire. So you're not a saint and you're under attack and why the heck is it so bad for you to want to feel a little vindicated, a little avenged, a little... in control?

Don't do it.

That brief sense of satisfaction you'll undoubtedly enjoy will fade quickly... but the regret you'll feel for sinking so low will last the rest of your life.

Don't offer the bait.

Don't take the bait.

For your sake.

Get over it

When you forgive somebody, it doesn't necessarily mean you want to invite them to your table.

—Oprah Winfrey

Anxious about demons getting unleashed when you break up?

Of course you are. You're going to get a raw deal. Screwed over. Lied to. Betrayed. Ripped off. Manipulated. Bullied. Humiliated. Treated with contempt.

Should I go on?

I should. Because you don't know the half of it yet. When you end a serious relationship a new world of scumbags probably will emerge. Your ex? Out for blood. Friends may turn on you. Your own family may stun you with indifference—worse, they may side with your ex. And just when you think you can't get more thrashed, the bell rings: It's round two of a nine round bout.

But if you're exiting an unhappy relationship it's all for the good. No matter how intense the transition, it's still better, still worth it, to break up, move on and be done.

And luckily there's a time-tested coping strategy for radically reducing break up stress and pain:

Get over it.

Forgive them. All of them. Everyone.

And, now.

I speak from experience. Some really shitstorm divorce stuff happened to me. And happened to pretty much everyone else I've spoken to who divorced or broke up a serious relationship. It's certainly possible to have a cheery, animus-free break up, but it's rare. To do so takes two partners *both* committed to keeping things friendly. Which is hard to sustain—if just one partner goes to a dark place, all sorts of genies get unbottled.

So while of course we should all try for an amicable disentanglement, we also need to prepare for some rough stuff. In short, train your mind, body and soul to *get over it.* Forgive all the assholes, the bullies, the shitheads who wrong you for no apparent reason. Let them go, packed up in the boxes in the attic of your soul containing the residues of the life you're leaving. Get over it, all of it, shed animosity or a desire for vengeance. Be assured, people will ding you emotionally, financially, physically, whatever. But screw them. Don't play the recriminations game.

I know, that's a *very* tall order.

Those *fucks.* They *fucking fucked* us.

True.

But here's another truth:

The goal—the *reward*—is breaking up, moving on, getting free, starting over. Starting a new life. And a "get over it" strategy gets you there faster, easier and with fewer balls and chains, slowing you down.

Now, I'm not advising you to be selfless. That would be too much to ask. (I couldn't do it.) No, I'm urging you to be *selfish*. Obsess on what's best for *you*:

Get done. And get going.

Besides, revenge is for wimps. Grudges are for cowards. For weaklings. Be strong. Get over it. Forgive them. All of them. Now. Before you even know who's doing you wrong or what's being done. Soon enough, you'll realize: That ability to get over it is actually *the very vengeance you seek*. Want to settle a score with so-and-so for doing such-and-such? Get over it. Forgive them. When you see them, say "Hello, how are you?" with a relaxed face as you calmly look them in the eyes. And so, emasculate them. Strip them of any hold they have on you. Your grudge, your lingering resentment is the only power they have over you. Take that away and crush those bastards.

Forgive them.

And consider: I 100% guarantee that, no matter what someone did or didn't do, over time, *eventually you will forgive them*. The cliche is true: time heals wounds—or at least, numbs and dims them until they recede so far into the irrelevant that they may as well be healed. True, we may never forget a slight, but no matter what, eventually we stop obsessing on it, ultimately life fills the holes in our hearts and patched up, we move on. Our lives constantly bring in so many new people and things that evolution burned in our DNA an essential survival mechanism—the ability to forget.

Thank you, evolution.

Believe me, this will happen to you. And it's *awesome*. Fantastic! Seriously—eventually we all tire of carrying the negativity-torch, exhausted by giving a shit about those *shits*. Moving on from that is like gulping fresh air after holding your breath.

So don't wait. Don't postpone joy, or delay liberty. Free yourself now.

If you're moving on, move on. Retribution is for losers— seriously, if you want those jerks to win, jump in the mud and start wrestling. Revisit over and over in your head every fight and acidic word, and what you'll say and do to make it all so correct when you get the chance.

Uh huh. Good luck with that.

When we let ourselves go to that place, the jerks *win*. Their manipulation is still manipulating. Want to be in control? To stop them being able to twist you up inside? Then stop letting those jerks stuff bad thoughts in your mind.

Granted, it's not easy. If you need a tool, try this: Pick your favorite song. Or a favorite vacation destination. Or a favorite meal. Or a favorite person. Those are your psychic bullets. Anytime an unwanted thought comes in your head—anytime you find yourself brooding, nursing some wound—load a psychic bullet in your psychic gun and shoot to kill: Switch to thinking about one of those super pleasant things. In that moment, that's your mantra. Stay focused there. Yes, initially it will feel forced. So what. Force yourself. You know how when you get some song you hate, maddeningly stuck in your mind? And you force yourself to hum or sing or focus on some other song that you like, to drive the crappy tune out of your thoughts? Yeah, do that.

I know, I make this sound simple and in reality it's amazingly difficult. And while I loudly preach the cause, honestly I can't claim to be a zen master myself. I sometimes find myself in the shower, not singing, not thinking ahead to my hopefully decent day, not forcing myself to think about my kids or my girlfriend or soup dumplings from my favorite restaurant, but brooding, over slights. Even ancient slights. Even slights by people I haven't heard from in decades. Even slights by people who are *dead* now.

Which is why I say: Revenge is for wimps. It takes no strength to indulge in vengeance fantasies. Wimps do it all day long.

What's the harm in revenge fantasies? It's huge. Life is a zero sum game. Your day is a zero sum game. Your mind, right now, is a zero sum game. (Meaning, it's a game where there's a winner and a loser, not a "win win.") If you're indulging in revenge fantasies, you're not spending that energy on anything else. Say, something productive or cheerful or that grows you as a person. No, you're indulging in self-pity. So in the zero-sum game, you're the loser. And by continuing to vex you, the target of your rage is the winner.

I'm not disputing you've been harmed. You have. Probably quite a lot. Here's your victim badge. You more than earned it. Just don't pin it on your chest? Stick it in a drawer. Bury it in the yard. It's like Kryptonite to Superman—it weakens you, makes you vulnerable, distracts you, freezes you in a time and place you want to leave behind. No matter who's involved or how mellow the circumstances may appear on the surface, when we break up a longterm relationship, inevitably we get victimized. *But we're not inevitably victims.* We're survivors, life-entrepreneurs, willing to take risks and do new things. Sometimes that means taking some vilification on the chin. But because we're survivors, we're prepared. Because we're entrepreneurs, we're not easily distracted from our true, hugely exciting missions and ambitions. Meaning:

We get over it.

We forgive them.

All of them.

Now.

Take the high road? The view's so much better.

Exercise

Make a *Shit List*.

Yes, really.

You need a computer, printer, paper, a hole punch and three ring binder. If preferred, a large pad of paper and pen will do.

First, unleash your rage: You're *really* going to make a *Shit List*. Your personal Book of Woe. Bible of Bile.

While I'm going to implore you to move on from your feelings of rage, sadness or frustration, I'm not going to ask you to pretend you're not genuinely feeling the hurt. Or that no one ever wronged you. We're all covered in scars and we can remember in agonizing detail how we got each one.

Write them down. One grievance per page. In the largest possible font, so each wound takes up an entire sheet of paper. Set margins so there's at least an inch on the left—you're going to print the pages and put them in the three ring binder.

Your Book of Woe.

Write as much as you like, but my advice is, keep each grievance super short. Write the headline, not the article. The details are all burned in your brain, right? Each printed out headline is an object symbolizing one grievance, not a full-on soul purge.

Spare no wrong. Create a page for the scumbag teacher who treated you like shit. The co-worker who sabotaged you. The back pain that hobbles you. The lover who dumped you. Whatever. Make as many pages as you need. There's no limit.

m all out. Each page should reveal itself to you at a
, triggering the appropriate flood of bad feelings. Use the
punch to insert them in your three ring binder. In whatever
rder you wish. Add more pages later. No requirement you get it
all out in one session.

But at some point, after you've added at least a few pages to the
binder, place the binder on a table in front of you and flip
through the pages.

There it is. Your *Shit List*.

Don't expect to suddenly feel liberated or enlightened. No
epiphanies here. But allow yourself to at least take a deep breath
and say, *Well. F***. There it is.*

Open the binder. Any page. Let yourself really wallow in anger,
self-pity, sadness or whatever comes. Don't hold back. Go there.
Whenever the moment passes, on the back of the page write the
date so you can track the times you were there.

Study your feelings a little. Are you still that enraged? Really? Or
does it maybe now feel a little... academic? You're justifiably
pissed off or sad but there's distance now. Some perspective.
Maybe the grievance is 100% real but isn't that burning anymore.

And maybe seeing all the pages in one place makes you feel...
lighter. Maybe even a little... silly. After all, how many grievances
are so intense, deep, raw and fresh they need to be revisited?
Who's in charge? You, or that grievance?

Maybe you're ready to forgive. Or at least, forget a little.

Then maybe, if you ever feel it's time, when some page just
doesn't feel that necessary anymore, just doesn't feel that raw or
important, tear that page out of the binder. After all, you control
the binder, it doesn't control you.

And there: You have forgiven.

Bless your soul, whatever, whoever that was, is no longer on The Shit List. No longer gets a precious place in your Book of Woe.

Meantime, you've justifiably acknowledged and named your legitimate feelings of anger about being poorly treated, by people, and by life, and by events. And you created a mechanism for you to be aware, and manage all that, and to add and subtract grievances when it's appropriate. And eventually, one day, maybe you realize you haven't bothered with it in a while, maybe in a long while, maybe somewhere along the way you just put it all away, for good, all is forgotten, just a dusty relic on a shelf.

Body

I do not want to be complicit in wiping myself out, and denying myself as a whole, broken-hearted, messy human being.
—Jerry Colonna

Sex

If sex is such a natural phenomenon, how come there are so many books about how to do it?

Bette Midler

Do you like sex?

If yes, jump ahead and skip the first short section here.

⟨⟩

Ok, so I guess you're saying you don't like sex.

Sorry but I'd like to question that.

Now, I 100% believe *you* believe that. And that you're speaking from the heart. And I concede, it's not impossible.

But I just think... maybe there's more to the story.

Of course, I don't know anything about you. Except one thing: you're here. So I gather you're in an unhappy relationship. And maybe you have ambivalent feelings about sex because of some of your life experiences. Maybe challenging or painful ones. My heart is so with you. One can't underestimate the lasting impact of these things, and the difficulty of feeling safe or comfortable again, or healed. So many things in life can make us feel tentative about sex, or apprehensive. I think every single one of us feels such things at various times in our lives. I certainly have.

But.

But.

I hope we can agree, when it's pleasing, sex can be one of the deepest forms of love, of vulnerable togetherness, a soul bridge to another, real emotional and physical connection, *true intimacy*. And a brief respite from the pervasive feeling we all struggle with: that, in the end, each of us are alone in the cosmos.

Why give up on *that*?

And yes, I think the issue is giving up. Respectfully, no one's forcing anyone to stop trying for a life with at least some happy intimacy.

Again, I don't deny there are people who really have no interest. But sex is sex is sex is sex—pretty much the entire human race has it on the brain, in the loins, in the DNA. From biology, evolution, culture, the media, whatever. People who lack interest are of course perfectly entitled to do so, and are just as likely to be terrific loving people as anyone else, but simple science tells us the urge—the *need*—to procreate is wired in our genes. So by definition, truly disinterested folks are a miniscule minority.

Which means: For almost all people, lack of desire isn't some unavoidable fate, some biological destiny. Rather, it's a reaction to an unfortunate accumulation of experiences, some unhappy rolls of the life-dice that wore the person down, or freaked them out, made them think the only manageable path is let go, give up.

But deep inside, maybe the sexual animal is just hibernating.

Also: For some folks, it's difficult to think physical unhappiness is itself reason enough to end a relationship. *How shallow. How immature!* So instead they convince themselves: *Whatever. No big deal. Sex just isn't that interesting to me.*

Is either possibly you? That you *think* you don't like sex but well, maybe you don't really know and maybe, just maybe, actually, you do? Or maybe you don't have enough varied personal experiences to truly evaluate your feelings—you're overwhelmed by an unhappy situation and you don't know what you don't know? Or you're just uncomfortable or embarrassed to even think sex is all that important?

No matter.

Your sex life is not over.

If that's what you want.

As billions of humans can attest, confusion about sex and lack of sexual fulfillment is stupendously common... but not fatal. It's a temporary, solvable condition.

Solvable by fixing a relationship...

...or ending it.

Yes, only you can decide to stay or go. And I don't know your situation. But I do know, enjoying intimacy with another human, who you want to be with and wants to be with you... well, that's one of our brief human life's great treasures. Giving up on that when it's still possible, well, if you want my hard-boiled advice—actually, even if you don't—it's this:

Don't give up.

Keep trying. Don't assume you know everything. Or even know anything. Even about yourself. All that matters is, sex is a natural part of life. Just like eating. And breathing. And emotions. So don't give up eating. Don't give up breathing. Don't give up loving.

Don't give up seeking intimacy.

And yes: love is the answer, love is the ultimate—but in consenting adult relationships sex is an integral part of love. Sure we have sex without love. And love without sex. But sex *with* love, love *with* sex, well what superlatives *can't* be used to describe that?

So don't give up. Keep trying. You can start over anytime with a clean slate.

So I ask again:

Do you like sex?

⟷

(If you skipped ahead, jump back in here.)

A program like this is really all about sex.

It's about certain types of relationships—marriages, other serious commitments—that have one thing in common:

Sex.

Think of it this way: How many books, courses, articles and therapists are devoted to helping people manage *friendships*? Meaning serious relationships that are platonic, no sex. *Almost none.* And how many are devoted to helping people with relationships that involve intimacy?

Billions.

Sex is the key.

There's a vast difference between relationships involving intimacy versus ones without it. And that's sex. Take away sex and marriage is pretty much just a friendship with a business contract.

Consider: If sex is good (or even decent) somehow we much more easily and cheerfully endure our partner's many annoyances and quirks. We feel a basic satisfaction that makes other grievances seem smaller. But when sexual discontent happens it colors things. And can heat other tensions to a boil. A relationship's success or failure often begins and ends in bed.

And I'm not just talking intercourse. By "sex," I mean snuggling, hand holding, making out, petting, grooming, personal appearance, scents, every physical thing that occurs, day in and day out, between partners. And it's not about "chemistry." Sexual happiness doesn't happen, it's made. Through commitment and work, not magic. Even after great beginnings many couples wind up alienated.

So then what? Whatever the roots of the unhappy situation may be, what should a person who feels sexually stymied do? Just keep trying? Keep working the same ostensible remedies over and over despite poor or no results?

No. That's a definition of insanity: doing the same thing over and over and expecting a different result.

So then just drop it, bury the feelings forever? Concede the relationship's always going to be physically unsatisfying so, alas, the intimacy side of life is just over?

No. That is simply not true, if you don't want it to be.

So if you feel sexually unfulfilled, first ask yourself plainly:

Do I think I can rekindle fulfilling intimacy in my relationship?

If the answer's "yes," well, ok then: Communicate, communicate, communicate. Change it up. Change everything up. Shed all shyness and embarrassment. Just do it. With a therapist present. On your own. Both. Talk—and listen—honestly. You have nothing to lose. And it's so worth it.

But if the answer's "no," or even "probably not"—if you've tried to address the situation with no success or the tension has festered so long it's hard to remember anything else—then ask yourself another plain question:

How important is intimacy to me?

If the answer's anything other than "zero," you're on to the most difficult question:

Is staying in my sexually unhappy relationship worth it?

My answer is, no. It's not.

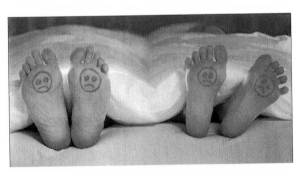

Remember: As a biological, chronological matter, the possibility of sexual fulfillment is not over for you.

Today, science allows us to enjoy our physical selves much longer, and with much more intensity, than at any time in history. Science and medicine have basically beat biology. Old age lost. So many things are now possible for so many more people, so much longer. Exercise, diet, health care, Viagra—we can snuggle and hump ourselves into exhaustion, well into what used to be considered doddering old age. Check it out: Today's retirement communities are happy dens of iniquity. (Healthy ones, too—sex is good exercise.)

So lucky you, modern human. You were born at the right time. There's little if anything physiological preventing you from pursuing the intimacy you want.

<⊞>

And don't feel guilty because you're a horny human.

Horny is healthy. Horny is normal. To say one has sex on the brain just means, one has a brain.

And yet we do feel guilty. Ten thousand years of religious, societal and cultural traditions have a strong pull. And we reflexively seek to avoid the critical opinions of others around us.

Is that a factor for you? In addition to all the stuff *inside* your heart and head, do you feel *external pressure*, too?

Let me let you off that hook, if I can. I think adhering to traditional ideas about sexuality just because they *are* traditional is itself an antiquated, obsolete idea and it's continuing presence in our modern lives is driving us all a little *nuts*.

Most importantly, I don't see how denying our basic human-ness due to cultural or social pressure leads to more happiness. And isn't seeking a little happiness in our brief time on Earth what life is all about? I think so. As long as our pursuit of happiness doesn't cause others pain or suffering, it should take priority. For me anyways, caring about what others do or think about sex has zero priority.

In any case, keep in mind most traditional sacred texts advocate all sorts of things we reject in the modern world. Slavery, for example. Judaism, Christianity, Islam, Hinduism, Shinto, Native American and other indigenous peoples' cultures all practiced slavery in early times, so their ancient sacred texts bless it. But naturally we ignore that. So why care about old thinking about intimacy?

Now I'm not going to argue for or against marriage, monogamy or fidelity. The morality and utility of such things is *not* one size fits all. Such deeply personal matters are up to you.

But when it comes to sex, traditions don't matter. And the past doesn't matter. Your past. Society's past. Religion's past. What you "believe" needn't matter. Or thought you believed. Or what you think everyone else believes. We should approach sexuality with the same willingness to innovate and adapt as we do so many other important things. No tradition contemplates cell phone etiquette—we're making that up as we go. The Buddha may have achieved enlightenment but the wisdom of using jets to fly salad greens to our dinner tables, well, we're on our own.

Which, as a practical matter, means:

Your sex life isn't over, if that's what you want.

And if that means you have to end an unhappy relationship, do it. Lack of intimacy, lack of sex is as good a reason as any.

There's no guarantee you'll get what you want, but there *is* a guarantee you *won't* get it if you don't keep trying. And to keep trying you need a partner you want to be with physically, and who wants to be with you. Is that who you're with now?

One more time: If you've been told—*or are telling yourself*—a fulfilling sex life is over for you, or you need to suppress yourself for some greater good, sorry, no, that's not true.

Actually, not *sorry*. *Happily*, that's not true.

None of this means disrespect your partner.

Or abandon or deceive anyone. If you decide to move on, awesome, go for it, but with fairness, respect and openness.

Maybe you've already talked the sex subject to death and it's way past time to move on to other topics. But maybe you haven't really had an open discussion about sex. If so, your partner at least deserves to know you're unhappy and why. *F*** it, get a divorce* doesn't mean, f*** over your partner. (Even if you want to. Especially if you want to.)

Tread delicately. We all do feel intimacy issues more deeply than other tensions. Assume your partner is as sensitive, confused and vulnerable as you. No recriminations. No expectations of apologies or assigning guilt. All is forgiven. And nicely ask them to extend you the same courtesy. The past is the past. For the purpose of this conversation with your partner, you are as much at fault as they are, whether that's true or not, and the sex discussion is about offering to explain some of what went into your decision to break up, not to catalog what anyone did or didn't do, or make anyone get defensive. The goal is to get on a new path, but not by trampling anyone.

It's not that we're failing monogamy. Monogamy is failing us.

—Dan Savage

Finally, a word on "infidelity."

If there's been infidelity, cheating, or whatever you call it, in your relationship—either by you or your partner— don't go down the rat hole of histrionics.

Was there malicious intent? Was anyone out to deliberately hurt anyone? Or did the transgressor feel trapped, unfulfilled, unhappy, and acted on that, and the real offense committed was silence—keeping those feelings and actions hidden.

Was it even a secret, really? Did the betrayed partner really have no idea there was such dissatisfaction? Were both parties guilty of silence?

Maybe the betrayed partner genuinely believed everything was great until an anvil fell on their head. But even if that's you, try to rise above. Don't get distracted. What's done is done. Focus on what you want to happen now. And tomorrow. Stay together? Break up?

Has trust been damaged? Of course that can be devastating. But stay calm. If you decide to break up, the sexual trust issue is, well, moot.

And if you're the "cheater," own it. You were sexually unhappy to the point of acting out. You can't take it back and maybe you don't even want to. But no recriminations. Your partner didn't do anything wrong or force you to do anything. And your partner is suffering. So maybe you don't apologize for your *actions*—no shame about unfulfilled sexual longing—but intentionally or not you hurt your partner. Apologize for *that*. And mean it.

If you're the aggrieved party, and the relationship is breaking up, try not to complicate the disentanglement with rage. Raging and punishing feels good for a minute or two but in the end, achieves nothing and deepens and prolongs the agony, and your break up. If your partner wants to try to explain, listen, you may learn something. If it feels like a waste of time, or rationalizations or accusations, breathe deep and let it go, you're still the aggrieved party and words can't change that. So be civil and move onto more important topics—say, the ending of your relationship.

The bottom line is, whether you're the "cheater" or the aggrieved partner, focus on the future. Our pasts are always complex messy stews, subject to endless review and reinterpretation. But the future is wide open and unwritten. Most of the time, so-called "cheating" is a symptom of something bigger. Is it worth digging into such things as part of breaking up? *Are* you breaking up? Or looking to stay together? Decide.

"Infidelity" is just a sign of an unhappy relationship. Don't stay in an unhappy relationship. Only you can set you on a new path that maybe offers more happiness. And that starts with a basic decision: I'm moving on.

◄II►

I'll close with a little etymology—the study of the origins of language.

Today, the word "libido" means sex drive. Its roots are in the old Latin words *libido* and *lubido*, which mean desire, eagerness, longing, passion, lust. Makes sense. But "libido" also traces back to a much more ancient word, *leubh,* that appears all over the globe, in Sanskrit, Persian, Slavonic, Lithuanian, Old English, German and elsewhere.

Figured it out?

Say it out loud:

Leubh.

Love.

Yup, "libido" has the same really ancient root as "love."

I don't care who you are or where you come from or what your situation is.

You deserve libido. You deserve love.

Exercise

Part 1: *The Libido Meter*

Strap yourself into my cool new invention *The Libido Meter*.

This ingenious (imaginary) device is to your libido what an EKG is to your heart, a quick check of your overall condition.

(Everyone passes, with flying colors. And there's no bad news.)

To start, close your eyes and imagine the best sex you ever had. Actual sex, a real encounter you had with a partner, or multiple ones, or just pleasuring yourself. With your current significant other or someone else, doesn't matter—as long as it's the best sex you ever had. And it doesn't matter whether anyone else would consider it great sex. All that matters is what you think.

Does recalling that make you horny? Be honest. Rate yourself on *The Libido Meter*, 0 to 10: Zero, you're completely unmoved. Ten, you have to go masturbate right now.

Write down whatever details made it the best. Be specific. The way he used his tongue shocked me and made me go nuts. The way she cried out so loudly, wow. Or the evening was perfect, dinner, champagne, cabin by the lake, we're alone, in love...

If conjuring up that episode and details made you horny, is that a feeling you recognize? Whether from sex or fantasizing, do you feel it often? Or is feeling horny a kind of reawakening, a lust you haven't felt in a while. Use *The Libido Meter*: Zero, you'd forgotten what horny feels like. Ten, no matter what you feel horny every day.

If imaging the best sex you ever had does *not* make you feel horny, that's fine too. But ask yourself, is it just general disinterest, or is there a specific reason? Maybe you were high on ecstasy during that "best" encounter and while it was great then, now you have no interest in that stuff. Or maybe the sex was super but the partner turned out to be an ogre and that turns you off. Or maybe you just don't feel like reawakening sex feelings.

There are no right or wrong answers. The point is, try to evaluate how far from everyday lust you are at this point in life. And whether that's something you'd change if you could. Because you can. Your sex life is not over.

<⏸>

Next, while you're still strapped in *The Libido Meter* think about this: For your birthday, your partner surprises you and says, *Baby, drop everything. Right now. We can do anything, money's no object, we have all the time in the world! What should we do?*

Whatever your answer is... how does sex fit in? And how much does the fact I made the fantasy revolve around your current partner influence that? Honesty, please. What if it was Denzel Washington or Matthew McConaughey offering a birthday fantasy? Or Scarlett Johansson or Beyonce? Or any human of your choice? Would your feelings be different? If given the chance to think freely, without guilt or judgement, about how you feel about sex, separate from your current relationship, how do you feel about it?

Part 2: Sex Robot

To thank you for helping me test *The Libido Meter*, I have a gift: My startup created the perfect sex robot. No one can tell it's not human. We have male, female, black, white, tall, short, skinny, curvy, whatever. And all programmed to perfectly mimic human actions and emotions. They laugh and cry and though they have no biological need, they occasionally excuse themselves to "use the bathroom" and at night they "sleep." And they have the same odors and messes as humans. And they enjoy sex. Or don't, if that's what you want. They do, or don't do, anything you ask.

I'm giving you one. (Or more than one if you like.) Just tell my startup what you want your robot to look like. And *be* like. Gentle and sweet? Macho? (Kinky or rough play is safe. You can instantly turn off a robot by saying, "Robot, shut down.")

OK, you have your robot. Please give it a name. (Seriously. It's not furniture. As you'll quickly learn, it mimics humans so well, and learns so naturally, you'll forget it's inanimate.) For now, I'll use John/Jane. Describe what sexual activities you want John/Jane to do. And what *you'll* do to please John/Jane—my startup's engineers are so brilliant they made John/Jane feel pleasure, even orgasms. You'll quickly want to make John/Jane enjoy sex as much as you do. It's so much more... human.

Remember, this is all top secret, no one will ever know a thing, no one can get hurt, and if you accidentally damage a robot, no prob, you get a replacement no charge.

Does thinking about what you'll do with your gift excite you? Enough so that maybe you feel a little encouraging motivation to try to get some real libido gratification back in your life? After all, if you don't want it to be, your sex life is not over.

Pruning

Imagine no possessions. I wonder if you can.
—John Lennon

We're spirits, in the material world.
—The Police

When serious relationships break up, not only do our emotional universes change, but our whole *material* world gets shaken up as well. Many people let fear of such real-world disruption paralyze them.

Fear of material change is normal but it's not a reason to lock in to an unhappy relationship. No matter how much we worry or resist, things and people come and go. It's a healthy and constructive aspect of human life.

If you break up your unhappy relationship, your personal physical world will likely, literally, change. Your home, maybe. Your car, maybe. Your clothes, your haircut, your favorite restaurants and hangouts. Your routines.

Your friends, maybe. Maybe even your closest friends.

Your family. Or people you used to think of as family, but realize, aren't.

Big seismic changes. Pretty rapid, sometimes.

So it's worth it to think ahead. Do a little preparation for the disruptive yet natural evolution in your physical reality.

Or if you're still on the fence about breaking up, to do a little consideration—to factor in such changes into your decision.

For most of us, there's good news here too, a silver lining—the chance to *physically get a fresh start*, relief from stuff and even people that, perhaps with good intentions, have bogged us down.

No matter what though, breakup time is a time of pruning.

⟨⊪⟩

To begin to wrap your brain around such material world changes in a relationship breakup, try to embrace that this will happen at all. You can't make a huge change in your universe and not have there be ripple effects. You can't just point your mouse at your significant other and click the delete key and have everything else just remain nicely and comfortably in place.

But again, such disruption does not have to be a negative. If you're a parent, you know the arrival of a new baby changes everything, including everybody's material world, as all sorts of new places, things, arrangements and people rush in. Breaking up your unhappy relationship is the birth of a new you, a rare, precious opportunity to have a fresh start in a new world full of new people, places and things. It's not a zero sum game, with a clear winner and loser. Though big changes abound, and some things and places and even people will inevitably be left behind, your old life does not have to "lose" for your new life to "win." You can have peace in both.

In short, it's perfectly ok to prune. And be pruned.

⟨╫⟩

Ever rolled up your sleeves and finally got around to cleaning out that closet? Or garage? The work sucked. Dusty sweaty labor.

But remember how *good* it felt to actually be rid of all that stuff, to the point where, once done, you chide yourself for thinking you ever felt you needed all that *junk*.

Pruning.

When you move on from a relationship, that's what happens.

Whether you want it to or not.

For one thing, you'll part ways with all sorts of possessions, and acquire new ones. When you break up, all that stuff you and your partner live surrounded by today must get divided up. You can't just take it all. Neither can your ex.

So out comes the samurai sword... and *slice*.

Some of it's just flotsam and jetsam, happily discarded. Some of it, though, will be precious, or necessary. So fasten your seatbelt. Relationship-is-over pruning will definitely entail a lot of work, and maybe some heart-wrenching decisions. At times it may just... suck.

And then there's the shock of the new—in a relatively short time, why, you may barely even recognize the stuff of your life. Because it's all so *new*. Foreign. Until one day, it becomes yours. Your stuff. Melts into being *you*, as stuff does. And that old stuff that seemed so precious? Memories dim, often to a complete blank. Remind me: Why did I care so much about that mirror?

But meanwhile, post breakup, you'll have started to put down new roots, build a new nest, map yourself onto your new surroundings and stuff. Congratulations. For most of the human race, that's a fantastic thing—and all too rare. For most of us, the last time we did anything at all that fresh, new and invigorating was maybe when we got married or hooked up longterm, and settled into a new life. Or had kids. But since then, through nobody's fault, it's been a routine, even sedentary life. With that creeping paralysis that somehow settles in, that resistance to, sometimes fear of, big change and the unknown. Culminating in a fairly monotonous, day in, day out life, where years and even decades melt away, until finally we make that one hugely disruptive "new life" move that can't be resisted: to a nursing home.

Or a funeral home.

But not you.

Post breakup, despite all the challenges and pratfalls, I suspect you'll be excited and empowered to find yourself still very much alive and kicking. Open to change, liberation, and the closure of an old relationship that, let's face it, was once fresh air in your lungs but hadn't made you feel alive and inspired in ages.

So you took the plunge. You moved on.

And it may take a while but one day, you'll look around your new life and surroundings and think:

Holy moley, I did it. I literally moved on.

And also:

Gosh, I'm scared. But also proud. And happy—I really am still capable of reinvention. I'm still alive and kicking.

But I'm jumping the gun. We haven't talked yet about the really hard part of rupturing your material world.

Most challenging, when you move on from a relationship you'll also prune *people*.

Or they'll prune you.

Ouch.

And you'll acquire new people.

Yikes. Strangers.

Sorry, but it happens to us all.

Naturally you're feeling anxious now. What's more important, more essential, more comforting, more the true stuff of our lives, than our human relationships, our peeps? I mean, you only want to break up with your soon-to-be-ex, right? Not with all your friends. Not with family.

Sorry, it happens. Whether you're the driver or not. Odds are high that, say, a year after your break up—maybe less, maybe a lot less—your everyday social interactions will be very different than they are today. A different set of characters, relationships, dynamics, routines.

But then, over time—and similar to the material stuff—this people-pruning process will become less scary, then not at all scary, then intriguing, interesting, then, yes, we can admit it—fun, even a gargantuan relief, and, yes, let's say it—a reward.

A *benefit* of your break up.

Yup, you won the Freedom Prize: freedom from various people and relationships that, upon honest reflection, may have been sweet and nice, even deep, meaningful and important, but now, going forward, in your new world, are not really all that important or special or beneficial anymore. *Not worth saving.*

And certainly not worth staying in that unhappy relationship for.

That is, ripe for pruning.

Pruning in a gentle, kind way, of course, where no one is intentionally hurt. For once you are ensconced in your new world, you'll see that those kind, loving people were, in fact, also unwitting anchors tied to you, limiting your growth, movement and reinvention.

Or maybe limiting your *fun*.

It's perfectly ok to place a priority on having fun in your new life. Especially if, in your old life, in your old unhappy relationship, you felt fun was lacking.

In your new world, you will find it daunting and frustrating, but also fun and thrilling, to meet new people and forge new relationships. It ain't going to be easy. But it is going to be awesome. The very core, the very reason, the very basis for why you decided to break up in the first place: to move on to a new life. A new life of new things places and yes, people. But it's hard to do that when you allow inertia or fear to compel you to just keep seeing and interacting with the exact same people, day in and day out—dragging your past around with you, hampering your new life from becoming, well, *new*.

Prune, baby, prune.

<+++>

Again, no offense to all the wonderful things, places and people who drop off your radar then out of your life.

They're frigging awesome. How do I know? Because you selected them to be in your life before. I trust your judgement.

But some of those things, places and people are just not the particular right awesome for your awesome new life. Not anymore.

And seriously, this is not "putting lipstick on a pig." Pruning can at times be painful, sure, but it is always a natural, helpful, even restorative process. It's an acceleration, a healthy amplification of what we all do, or aspire to do, every single day: evolve and change.

Of course, yes, when losing friends, family and colleagues it's natural to feel sadness, fear, anger and trauma.

But it's not the *result* of the pruning process. It *is* the pruning process. Feel those feelings. How can we not? You parachuted into the wilderness and it's super scary. But darn it, lace up your hiking boots, grab a machete and start hacking a trail. And take a look around—the wilderness is gorgeous, ripe with sustenance and opportunity.

<+++>

Bear in mind, by resisting pruning you're not doing yourself or anyone else any favors. Or avoiding the inevitable.

For example, whether it's true or not, many of your peeps are going to feel they have to choose sides, they can't be friends with both you and your ex. Admit it, you've done that yourself.

People are going to prune *you*.

They're not trying to hurt you.

But it may hurt.

Why, I'm in the throes of a personal crisis! I'm broken, so vulnerable! Why is so-and-so abandoning me?

Well, maybe they're taking sides. Choosing your ex. Or maybe they're unsure how to act, uncomfortable being around someone in a mess. They're busy and stressed themselves—who has time for *your* mess?

Or maybe they never were as close to you as you thought. And they're pruning.

Whatever.

Stuff happens.

Mentally go through your friends. And yes, your family. And your ex's family. Do you care if they choose your ex? Do you maybe in fact hope they *do*, so without saying a word you can happily release them from your orbit?

For me, the best scenario is where a person takes some ownership of the process and actively sorts the wheat from the chaff, and prepares for come what may, and one way or another cuts loose from people and things that, if one is honest, should be. Or have to be.

And by the way, "cutting loose" can and often should be done passively.

Don't call people and tell them they're off your list. Just resist the urge to proactively try to recruit people to your side, or work yourself into a lather, making dates with people who, really, you're indifferent about, or who seem indifferent about you, and all just to try to keep up appearances, or keep some peripheral relationships alive while your breakup is making you feel adrift.

Instead, just go quiet. See who reaches out to you. See who doesn't. See who you really, really do want to see, for comfort or counsel or giggles. Focus on them. Everyone else? Whatever. Give yourself a good long time of pretty much doing nothing— eventually you'll know who got pruned and who didn't, and who pruned you.

And don't get sore. No anger, no grudges, no urgent need to set the record straight. Very quickly, none of that matters. Just assume it's all good. It has to be. It can't be undone. And besides, you have an exciting new life to tend to...

<hr>

Of course, if you decide to *actively* prune, terrific. Go for it. Your breakup is a get-out-of-jail-free-card—to be reclusive or hard to schedule or whatever you feel like. Get-out-of-jail-free-card, meaning, in your time of breakup, no one will accuse you of being cold or cruel, just human, in the throes of a massive life change. So go on declining invitations from people you want to prune. Encourage people to reach out to your ex and offer them solace—you'll be perceived as being selfless and kind while pruning that person by gently aligning them with your ex.

Or just... disappear. No guilt, no looking back, no obligation.

Remember, if people really are your friends, they'll allow you a wide berth. They'll be respectful. In short, they won't be bruised if you retreat from the scene. And if, at the end of that retreat, it turns out your routine of seeing them has faded, well, life happens. No harm done. No hurt feelings. See you on Facebook.

Or never.

And if they're not your friends:

Prune.

Exercise

Part 1: No Possessions

Imagine no possessions.
I wonder if you can.

In his world famous song *Imagine*, John Lennon wrote and sang those words as a loving challenge to humanity.

Well, ok then: Imagine no possessions. I wonder if you can.

Breaking up and moving on almost always involves the large scale pruning of one's stuff. So take a moment. A deep breath or two. And visualize—how would it feel to quite literally start over with no possessions?

It could happen.

Very unlikely, but not impossible.

Would you stay in your unhappy relationship if the cost of breaking up was starting over with no possessions?

In any case, the only way to break up and move on relatively quickly, and really be free to start anew, is to not argue about *stuff*. If your soon-to-be ex is in a fighting mood or wounded frame of mind, they may want to squabble about everything. Every spoon. Maybe even your clothes—if, for example, rightly or wrongly your ex claims to have paid for all of it.

Imagine no possessions.

I'm not saying *expect* no possessions. It's super unlikely.

But just, imagine. As extreme prep for going through an extreme breakup with a nevertheless clear head and eyes on the prize—

your ability to move on. Imagine the perfect storm: You start with some clothes and not much more.

Is that such a disaster you'd rather stay in your relationship?

The cliche holds true: Hope for the best, plan for the worst.

Imagine no possessions. I wonder if you can.

Part 2: Some Possessions

So you've just visualized the worst case. Good work. Now, relief:

Imagine *some* possessions.

Do a massive, pretend-prune of all the stuff in your life.

It's just an exercise. Change your mind a million times. The point is to work out your pruning muscles and see how it feels. Form an opinion by mock-doing, not by avoiding even thinking about it. For though "no possessions" is unlikely, "some possessions" is almost guaranteed. When you move on, you'll need to divide up the mountain of stuff you share.

Ever thought about that as a practical matter?

Are you ok with such and such *stuff*—and so and so *thing*—disappearing from your life? Or ending up with your ex? What are you prepared to do, trade, sacrifice?

Does this thought make you anxious? Or, does mock-pruning make you feel relieved, even elated, that that *thing*, or that *person*, will be disappearing? It's perfectly ok to feel that way. Welcome to the club.

So grab your computer or a pad and pen. You're now going to wander through your residence (your life!), every room, the basement, garage, attic, closets, cabinets, drawers, bathrooms, everywhere—and make lists of possessions. And you're going to unleash your Samurai sword and slice everything into three piles:

1. What I *must* have.
2. What my (soon to be) ex will say he/she must have.
3. The "Limbo List": Stuff I probably don't care much about and not sure my ex will either.

Ok, begin. Try to be at least somewhat comprehensive—catalog as many possessions as can even remotely be considered shared property and assign each a number, using those categories.

Don't do running tallies or stop to try to think about the big picture, until you're done.

But then, do stop and think about the big picture:

a) Have I been honest? Do I really give a darn about my "must have" list? Am I willing to deviate from what could be an amicable break up to fight over this thing or that thing? Can my soon-to-be ex and I possibly try to "have our cake and eat it too"? For example, the wedding album. What if we both want it? Can we make a digital copy? What if neither of us wants it?

b) Have I inadvertently been too provocative? Will some aspect of my division of stuff into piles provoke my soon-to-be ex into rage? Is it worth it?

c) Has my division come out roughly fair, at least as far as money goes? If we roughly but honestly appraise my piles by their monetary values, will either I or my soon-to-be-ex owe the other one money to compensate for a disparity in the piles' values? Is that worth it?

Regarding c)—A quick note on how that works.

An example: If you "must" have all the jewelry and the nice new TV and computer and the nice new car, and your ex's "must" pile just has a bunch of old clothes, and a junker older car, well then, you're going to need to together come up with some kind of appraisal or honest guess as to the values of your two piles, and you'll need to pay him for your half of what you are taking away.

The math:

Let's say that, together, you as a couple own one nice new TV, which you paid $1,000 for. You feel you "must" have it, and your ex doesn't object as long as you compensate him accordingly. It's a year old, not brand new so you argue it's worth less than $1,000. Your ex concedes the point. But it's still in mint condition and to replace it would cost $1,000. So maybe you and your ex agree it's now worth $800. Ok, you then owe your ex $400. Why not the full $800? Because you already owned one half of that TV. You are only buying your ex out of the one half of the TV *he* owned.

Get it?

Now put your big list away for at least a full day.

Then take it out again and review it with fresh eyes. And revise.

Eventually, emotion will fade and you'll have a hopefully simple, sane view of how to prune all that stuff if/when the time comes.

Dating

My philosophy of dating is to just fart right away. —Jenny McCarthy

Do you cringe at the idea of having to date again? Does the thought of being single once more fill you with dread?

That's natural. But it's no reason to stay in a bad relationship. If that's holding you back, good news:

Meeting people today is easy. Want to date? You will.

↔

It's so common to worry that when we break up we'll be at a loss as how to meet new people, so we'll end up alone. Making it tougher, for many of us, our younger, first go-around in the world of dating was cringe-worthy—dumb fumbling around or a boozy blur that was exhausting then and would kill us now, or just a lot of disappointment and tedium.

Who would want to do that again?

Actually, you would, after you take a look at *modern* dating.

It's an entirely different world now. A much better one, a friction-free digital marketplace where meeting people is about as tough as using Amazon.com. If anything, the difficulty now is *oversupply*—it's so easy to meet people online, scarcity of opportunity has been replaced by a teeming zoo parade that at times needs fending off. The challenge is finding the *right* people, in a sea of folks waving and calling, *Hi, look at me.*

But if you can use a phone, you can do online dating. Most services are free, or charge small fees to access premium features. Gone are the days when it was necessary to sit on a barstool hoping that—completely randomly—a new, pleasing face will walk in and be attracted to you, and you'll get in a conversation that has a little magic. Or get tipsy and hop in bed for a little sweaty fun, hoping afterwards you'll genuinely like your partner. Websites, apps, texting, video chat, swiping and algorithms crafted to find like-minds—all have made those pre-digital mating rituals obsolete.

At minimum, you'll meet people you're comfortable to connect with a little. There's no risk beyond a bit of your time. No more dressed up, awkward dinners, where you get turned off in ten minutes then spend hours longing to escape. With digital dating, if, where and when you meet people in real life is up to you. If you have hesitation there's no need to go anywhere or do anything. First dates can (and probably always should) be light, daytime meetings at busy coffee places, just a brief, safe opportunity to see if the real person measures up to the online profile. (And allow them the same courtesy.)

Again, none of this means you'll find true love quickly or at all. I have no idea of your standards, or whether you brush your teeth or use deodorant. But I do know, if you want to date, whether seeking just one special someone, or playing the field, or just window shopping, it's all just a click or tap away.

⟨⊪⟩

Digital dating is not a niche anymore—it's the most mainstream, common way singles meet. Whatever stigmas may have existed years ago have vaporized. Recent numbers are astounding. According to the parent company of Match.com (which also owns Tinder, and many other big digital platforms,) in 2017, 550 million people used online dating services. Match.com *alone* gets 59 million visitors *every month.*

If you have a specific focus, there are services which slice and dice humanity in various ways:

- Bumble — Only women can initiate contact
- eHarmony — Special process to predict compatibility
- Happn — Meet people you've crossed paths with already
- EliteSingles — Age 50+ preferred
- IndiaMatch — Indian preferred
- BlackPeopleMeet — African-American preferred
- ChristianMingle — Christian preferred
- JDate — Jewish preferred
- Muslima.com — Muslim preferred
- FreeThinkerMatch — Atheist/agnostic preferred

That's just a small sample. The list of specialized services is long. Whatever flavor human you seek, ye shall find.

⟨⊪⟩

Of course, with digital dating comes another distinctly modern task: Presenting ourselves online. For we, too, are in that vast sea of people saying, *Please look at me.* Today, before we can hope to make someone love us as a *person*, we first have to get them to engage with us as a *persona*, a digital profile, snippets of text, data, pictures and videos.

Yes, people lie. Post 10 year old photos. Pad resumes. Exaggerate wealth or status. When you check out someone online and discover they led you on, you'll be mad. But you'll also be mystified: Sure, they may be trying to con you in some bad way, but more likely, they're just *fools*, ridiculously hoping the fibbing that lured you in somehow won't bug you when you inevitably discover it's baloney. How many people stay attracted to someone they discover is a phony? Nevertheless, fibbers fib on, and weeding them out is an unavoidable nuisance.

Then again, online dating isn't a polygraph test or confession booth. We all have to decide where (if anywhere) the line falls between honesty and TMI (too much information). For example, unless it's an extreme situation, talking about one's eczema may not be necessary early on. We just have to decide as we go both what we offer up, and how we feel about what other people say or don't say. Personally, I think it's normal and OK to *not* disclose all warts right away. We all keep things to ourselves, every day, in real life. On the other hand, posting very old photos, or using heavy image retouching, or claiming to be much more affluent...

Maybe a good rule is, *Do unto others...* And keep an open mind. We all have to navigate the border between dishonesty and everyday mating ritual puffery. For example, it's probably ok to shave a few years off your age, and foolish to get upset when you meet people who do. If nothing else, that helps your profile show up in searches—if you're 50, you don't show up when people select the "40-49" search category. But those searchers probably don't care if you're 50. Or even a bit older. They didn't design the search parameters, some software engineer did. And if you want, you can come clean in the body text of your profile. Or quickly tell your real age to anyone who contacts you. Or never say a word because you're confident you look younger and if, after a few dates, you really like someone, you'll make full disclosure and hope it doesn't sour things.

Bottom line, I recommend honesty. If someone isn't interested in the *real* you, you need to know. And as the saying goes: The best lie is the truth because you can always remember what you said.

I know, this is all very well and good, but you're nervous. That's understandable. You're older now. Tired. A little overweight, maybe. With work, kids, debts, a wrinkle or two and body pain. But so what. *The same is true of the multitude of tired, flawed grown-ups who'd like to meet you.* You only want to date Brad Pitt or Gal Gadot? I guess *you* better look like Brad Pitt or Gal Gadot. Otherwise, congratulations, you're a normal human grown-up now. Warts and all. And while online dating hasn't eliminated the beauty contest aspects of mating rituals—a lot more on that subject below—it has made it wonderfully easy for people to connect on all levels, in a relaxed way, not just how one looks in a bar, or what can be shouted over music.

And presenting oneself online isn't some talent people are born with. It's a skill, acquired by practice and doing. Your first attempt will be just that, a first attempt. But you'll spend a little time, and you'll figure out how to talk about yourself and what pictures are flattering, and you'll browse other people's profiles and see what they do. And you'll probably *enjoy* it all—there's a genuinely fun, entertainment aspect to digital shopping for humans. (Beware: Human window shopping can be addicting!)

In any case, soon you'll find it all second hand. And you'll realize: While there's no guarantee you'll easily find *love* (and yes, there *is* one you'll find disappointments) the ease of searching and the size of the crowd saying *Hi, please check me out,* is just... amazing. Unless for some reason you choose *not* to, *you definitely will date,* and likely find someone (or many someones) you like. Hopefully, they like you. If not, rinse and repeat.

And don't forget: Another exciting new wrinkle about dating now is, you're so much more *you* now. You're not a kid anymore. Thank goodness. You're a more thoughtful, seasoned, smart, developed *you*. And you're aware of how *little* you knew about yourself and the world back when you were younger (and when you committed to your current partner.) Now, you know much more about yourself. And what you want.

So go find it.

> *I realized I'm not a person inside a body looking out. I am a body.*
> —Christopher Hitchens, *On Mortality*

Regarding those "beauty contest aspects of mating rituals"...

Before diving into the online dating pool in earnest, it probably behooves us all to take stock. You're out of circulation. Maybe out of shape. Maybe for years now you haven't cared much about a stepping-out wardrobe. Or, ahem, using a nose hair trimmer. You were in a lifelong relationship, why would it matter?

Now it does. It's sad but true—with humans, first impressions count. We don't get to show how witty and deep we are *inside* if our *outer* self doesn't attract. So maybe refresh and renew a bit?

I'm not suggesting you try to look like Tom Brady or Gisele Bundchen. You'll fail. (As would I.) But if you haven't primped for public consumption in a while, then doing so, at least a little, will pay dividends twice over. First, you'll look better. No downside. More importantly, it builds confidence, improves your aura in ways exercise, diet and fashion can't—by making you glow. Asked his most important job in World War II, Supreme Allied Commander (later President) Dwight D. Eisenhower said, *To smile.* Get your best smile back. And remember:

1) It's a marathon not a sprint.

Relax. There's no rush, no magic wand. Looking and feeling good is a lifelong endeavor. Start however you like. Make one or two small course corrections. Take a tiny step. Then another.

2) Exercise.

Leaving a long relationship is a trial for the body, not just the heart and soul. As Christopher Hitchens said: You *are* a body. Breaking up may beat you up a bit. Through obvious ways—sleeplessness, crazy eating—and subtle ones. You may get colds more. So train for your breakup, and to re-enter the dating world. Again, little stuff is fine. Walks. Stretching. Calisthenics. Bike rides. Pace when on the phone instead of sitting. Park your car far from destinations and walk back and forth. Take stairs not elevators. Pretty quickly small measures work wonders. And the minute you notice any improvement in your body, you'll understand how much good exercise also does for your *mind*.

3) Beware cravings.

Your body may hurt you by trying to escape stress and you may not even realize it. Like overeating. Occasional ice cream or chips are not only OK, they may be necessary to sanity. Enjoy. But regular overindulgences are very hard on health and looks. Six months of bingeing may take six years to recover. If ever.

Ditto alcohol. A divorced friend told me she didn't realize she was drinking so much until after she moved out. As a couple, she and her ex were "social drinkers," all good fun. But during the breakup, being loaded became how they managed to keep functioning around each other. Even after moving out, it was very hard to stop.

So when it comes to mind or body altering substances—food, alcohol, marijuana, pills, caffeine, tobacco, whatever—your breakup may be time to break up with that, too. Or ratchet down consumption. I know this is miserable advice—during a breakup we crave comfort and numbness. Maybe you can handle it. But maybe you can't. Err on the side of caution.

4) Mirror, mirror.

Do you look and feel now the way you want to when you're dating again? Be brutally honest. Maybe it's been stifling and horrible in your relationship. But it's also been liberating—from caring about your condition. You were attached forever, right? So what if your waistline changed. Or your hairstyle didn't.

It may matter now. Don't let inertia decide. Take a candid look in the mirror. You have the power to make changes, you just have to want to do so bad enough. And you may be a diamond in the rough, but you're still a diamond. You still have that awesome smile, sparkling eyes and sense of humor. You're an engaging, attractive animal, you just need grooming. So remember: *This* guy...

...became *this* guy:

Last, a cautionary note: If you haven't broken up yet, consider possible unintended consequences. If your partner doesn't know you're contemplating breaking up and you start preparing for dating, they may become wise. Your new attention to appearance may be a flashing sign saying you're leaving. Maybe that's a trigger that starts your breakup in earnest, ready or not.

But maybe that's ok. After all, there are 550 million singles online, eager for your arrival.

Exercise

Part 1

Download Tinder to your phone. Or Bumble, where only females can initiate contact. Or JSwipe if you want to meet only Jewish people. Or any dating app. Or all of them. They're all free, no cost to download and check out.

Just play around. Nothing serious, you're not really looking for dates yet. Just seeing what online dating is all about.

And go on Match.com web site. Just to window shop. Check out a bunch of other people's profiles. See what you find attractive, repellant or just boring. See the kinds of information people reveal (or don't) and what photos they publish.

Some mobile apps require you to log in using a Facebook account. If you don't have one, just go make one. There's no risk, you can delete it later if you really feel the need. Or make a profile with a phony name. And there's no need to put in lots of effort adding stuff to your Facebook profile. The dating apps need just the basics, like a birthday for age.

If you already have a Facebook account, if you use it to log in to a mobile dating app, your real name (from your Facebook account) may also be used in your dating app account. If that bothers you, go make a second Facebook profile with another name.

Part 2

Take the next step. Create an actual Match.com profile for yourself. No need to pay for the premium version of the site, unless you want to. If you use your real email address to create a fake profile, no problem, you can always redo the profile later.

(Though, note: some services do not allow a profile to switch genders once it is created.)

If you're really worried, ok, open Match.com on your computer but create your profile on a legal pad.

How does this feel? You probably haven't done this sort of thing in a long time, if ever. Do you have pictures of yourself you'd be happy to post? Practice taking some new selfies. And consider: what pictures of other people do you think are attractive? Smiling? Serious? Partying? Pictures with their kids? In bathing suits or revealing attire? Try taking some pics of yourself (or get help) which are expressly designed or organized for posting as a dating profile.

Soul

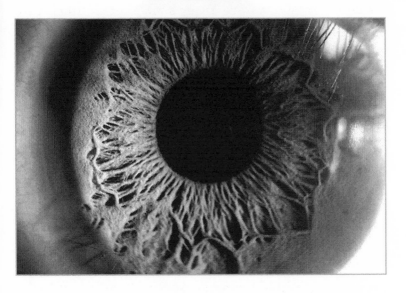

The world asks of us
only the strength we have and we give it.
Then it asks more, and we give it.
  —Jane Hirshfield
  The Weighing

Kids

Everybody knows how to raise children, except the people who have them.
—P. J. O'Rourke

Whenever I date a guy, I think, 'Is this the man I want my children to spend their weekends with?'
—Rita Rudner

I don't know if I believe in marriage. I believe in family, love and children.
—Penelope Cruz

For couples with children, "Because it's better for the kids" is always a big reason to stay in an unhappy relationship.

The thing is: *It isn't true.* It's *not* always better for kids if unhappy parents stay together. Years of scientific studies show: Kids of divorce can be just as happy and well-adjusted as those with married parents. Meaning:

Breaking up won't automatically hurt your kids or make you a bad parent.

Basically it depends on how progeny experience their parents breakup and behavior. If couples end relationships with civility, then remain amicable—at least, in front of the kids—the data shows little or no longterm negative effects on children.

Surprised? I was.

(By the way my definition of "child" is technical, not chronological. 2 or 32, all are"kids" here.)

(For more on the science, see the links at segment's end.)

‹‖›

I got divorced in Massachusetts. There, couples with kids must take a state-sponsored "parenting" class before the court will grant a divorce. I assumed it'd be like waiting in line at the DMV, but then, I really liked it. The learning was startling and inspiring: Scientists have studied divorce for years. Findings show the negative effects of divorce on kids are usually minimal. Children of divorce typically go on to have essentially the same happy or unhappy lives as kids of married parents.

So being "good" or "bad" parents is not tied to being a *couple*. Cheery married people can be awful parents. Frazzled singles can be great ones.

And *unhappy married folks*? I don't think we need much science to gauge that. Common sense says, when couples are miserable, their kids know—and usually are miserable, too. We should never underestimate how smart and perceptive kids are. They know they're in a painfully dysfunctional home. And no matter what, can it be *healthy* to spend years watching Mom and Dad fight, seethe or act cold and distant—or just plain loathe each other?

Of course, that's easy to agree with *in theory,* but super hard to act on in real life. It's just so painful, so terrifying when we look into our kids' faces, and start worrying about the maelstrom of breaking up, and think, *no, no, no, I just can't do that to them.*

But lucky us, we live in the modern world, where science can help. And again, the data's pretty clear: While parents breaking up does cause children short term stress and unhappiness, that passes, and needn't have long-term effects. Overall, both divorce and marriage kids have the same ups and downs in life: lengthy or brief relationships, breakups, depression, joy, success, bankruptcies, substance abuse, fame, wealth, crime, health, long or short life spans. They seek therapy in the same numbers, and the same percentages complain their parents screwed them up.

So, good news: If you're staying in an unhappy relationship just for the kids, you're off the hook. There's no need to feel that kind of pressure.

BUT.

There's cautionary data, too. *Some* kids *do* suffer long-term negative effects from parents breaking up. More frequent deep depression, for example.

Which ones?

Kids with parents who put them in the crossfire.

When splitting parents put kids in the middle they're much more likely to suffer painful long-term effects.

Huh. "Put kids in the crossfire?"

Who'd do that?

We all would.

If we complain to our kids about stress, the divorce, our ex.

If we take out our depression, rage or fear on our kid. Or in front of them.

If we use the kid to spy. Or try to turn the kid against our ex.

It we paint ourselves as a victim, made helpless by our ex's cruelty. (Even if it's true.)

If we openly use custody threats or bad parenting claims—again, true or not—as a weapon. (Don't fool yourself: Nothing stays secret, the kids will know.)

If we use a child to extract revenge or manipulate our ex. Or just to be mean.

If we blame our kid. For *anything*.

If we ignore our kid. Or disappear for a time. Or let our kid's routines suffer. Or let their world feel dirty and chaotic. (Do the dishes. And the laundry. Empty the trash.)

So recognize your early warning signs—any indications you're succumbing to the temptation to act out. Keep your *I'm-being-an-asshole-radar* on *high*.

And don't *ever, ever, ever* let a child believe for one second that somehow the breakup was caused by *them*.

It's natural for kids to wonder—*am I at fault*? So it's our job to make it just as natural for them to feel completely reassured—*no, no way is it my fault*. Because after all—*it isn't their fault, is it*?

⟨⊩⟩

Still wavering? Then remember: If 50% of marriages end in divorce (and, as I say in *By The Numbers*, I think the number's actually much higher) your kids—like *all* kids—are surrounded by people living in single-parent or non-traditional homes. It's all just... normal to them. So if you don't paint your breakup as freakish, or a nightmare, the kids won't either.

Know the old joke?

An old fish is swimming along. Two young fish swim by. The old fish nods, smiles and says, "Nice water today." The young fish smile back but when the old fish is gone, one young fish asks the other: "What's *water*?"

For kids today, divorce is water.

Yes, parents breaking up is a massive, painful earthquake for them. And yes, some kids may need special help, maybe with a therapist. But there's no shame in that, and help is readily available, and regardless, the essential point remains: A parental break up need not be a long-term injury, and usually isn't. The event is unfortunate, but it's not from outer space. Kids today are surrounded by non-traditional families in their social circles and the media. If everyone's committed to a reasonably amicable transition and evolution, the new life pretty quickly becomes the new normal, regardless of what came before.

And even if people *aren't* amicable, inevitably, things settle. No one *needs* to feel ashamed or like a freakish outcast. That's ancient history. *Unless we teach our kids to feel that way.*

So show the kids Mom and Dad can *be* apart but not *fall* apart. That the family dynamic is changing (and, in truth, is *always* changing) but their family is, and will always be, their family.

Easy?

No, *incredibly difficult*. This takes super-human self-control and constant diligence—and often saying and doing things that make you want to puke. Say, like praising your ex with a smile at the very moment he or she is treating you like *crap*.

But you can do it. Why?

Because they're your kids.

<HI>

Here's one way to keep kids out of the crossfire, feeling reassured: Invite them to be active participants.

Don't try to hide that a massive life change is going on. Have as few secrets as possible. Unless they're infants, your kids are smart and already intuit that everything is in play. So put it out there. But not in a judgemental way. No bad guys. No winners and losers. Just a family transition. Some marriages last forever, some don't, and unfortunately this one didn't. It's an emotional, complex *thing* to unwind for sure, and everyone's naturally feeling vulnerable and confused. But that's *life*: a gorgeous mess that isn't always fun. And because it's such a big complex transition, the kids input is welcome, super valuable.

Meaning: Ask the kids for help. Don't ask them to be judge or jury, or take sides or spy. Ask them to assist you and your ex. Bring them into the process of creating everyone's new lives. Now the family needs two residences, not one. Who lives where and when? That's usually the first question out of a kid's mouth after learning Mom and Dad are splitting. (*How and when to tell kids that is part of the Exercise for this segment.*) If you know the answer, explain. And say how you got that plan. And ask the kids if they agree that makes sense. Or how they might improve the plan. If you don't know who's going to live where and when, just say you don't. And ask the kids to help figure it out. Invite them to weigh in on where you move to. Apartment? House? This or that neighborhood? Walk to school? Bus? How about the kids' new rooms? Ask them if they want to decorate their rooms. Colors. Posters. Or any room...

The point is, there's a healthy, calm middle ground between painful silence about a split, and a war with kids in the middle. It's open acceptance of what's happening, acknowledgement that feelings are raw, professions of sympathy for the other parent (yes, feigned if necessary), and attempts to let the kids participate and have opinions—and see, first-hand, how modern, loving families deal with challenges. To *not* act like the world is coming to an end. Or that the family should feel ashamed or even unusual. And to make sure kids know, what *they* feel *matters*.

And of course, that *they did nothing wrong*. But they can do all sorts of things right. Like help Dad equip a kitchen during a confusing excursion to a store. Or offer that they've always wanted a bunk bed, and since they're moving, is that possible? Or promise Mom they'll help her manage her phone and computer.

When managed in a calm, amicable way, with ample communication and no vilification, the data shows: Children of divorce are not permanently disrupted by their parents breakup. Pretty quickly, things settle to a new normal, and the kids go on to live the same messy, wondrous lives as anyone.

As will *you*.

◄╫►

Which brings me to another important note:

While cutting your kids slack, cut yourself some, too.

Don't pretend you aren't confused, anxious or angry. You are. And while you do have to leave the kids out of it, and avoid the risk they'll feel hurt or responsible, that doesn't mean you have to try to be perfect. You'll fail. We all do. You're going to screw this up. Bad, sometimes. *And it's ok.* Your sanity and health depend not on perfection but on *reflection*. Taking the long view, seeing the big picture, stumbling and falling... and getting back up.

So get good at forgiving yourself—you'll need to do it often. Especially for slip ups with the kids. Stuff will happen. And it's ok. As long as you communicate with the kids that you screwed up and you're sorry, and move forward with a little cheer. And watch out for that horrible, downward spiral, where you temporarily lose your grip and mess up, or say something awful, or lose your cool. Which then makes you feel worse so you go deeper into funk... and lose your grip again.

Just forgive yourself. You didn't mean to muck up, did you? You're not perfect, you're a good person, in a storm. So acknowledge your frailty. Not some gusher confession of all your sins. Just a simple apology. It's a tough time, you lost your composure but you're back now and your ex—*the kid's other parent*—isn't Satan and the world isn't ending.

Most important, communicate that the kids aren't really the cause of the storm. Yeah, they spilled juice on the sofa, and broke a window, and got a bad grade, and drank the liquor. That's bad. And has to be dealt with. Maybe punished. But you overreacted and you're sorry.

Then move on. You have a huge load of responsibilities and people to care for. Don't neglect that by sulking or holding a grudge against yourself for not being perfect. The point isn't to try to protect the kids by putting them in some unbreakable, antiseptic safe-room for the duration. It's to make sure, amidst calm or chaos, that the kids know that divorce is a messy but common part of life, challenging to get through but everybody will, and one way or another will still respect and love one another. The family is reshaping, not blowing up.

At core, this is actually kind of simple, I think:

To manage kids just... love them. Openly.

By taking the high road, we teach our kids an immensely valuable lesson—how to handle life challenges with dignity, reserve and an open, forgiving heart. There's a better than 50/50 chance your kids will get divorced themselves someday, so make yours a lesson in how it can be done with class, and love.

And remember:

This mindset is great not just for kids but for *you too*.

You'll be happier leaving your kids out of the mess. You'll get huge pleasure seeing them not stressed in a time of stress. Seeing them just being kids. And you'll be happier seeing them *see you* as a calm, loving adult. Especially when *you* know you're barely holding it together.

This pays a dividend for the rest of your life. Well after the divorce, you'll discover your kids have a special, deep respect and love for you, as they come to realize how trying the divorce really *was* for you, but how nonetheless you took one for the team—*their team*.

So be selfish. Leave your kids out of your breakup, for *you*. Even when that means pretending to be warm to your ex.

Especially then.

◄◆►

A couple of last notes:

While I hope your soon-to-be-ex takes my program, probably they won't. So prepare: Your partner's behavior may be upsetting. When breaking up you may learn things you never suspected. Like, your ex views the divorce as liberation... from their own kids. They may not want to see them much. They may have other priorities, things that make your blood boil. Like partying. Or working 100 hours a week. Or having sex. Or maybe they reveal themselves to be petty, seemingly happy to give scant financial resources to divorce lawyers to fight over nothing, at the expense of their own kids.

You just have to deal with all that. And refrain from letting the kids know how you feel, or asking them to take sides. Or even to view your ex poorly.

But take heart. In the end you'll get what you want—your kids are smart, they'll know what's what. Maybe not on day one, but over time they'll understand the differences between their parents. As a friend counseled me: Over their lifetimes, *all* kids develop separate relationships with each of their parents. That's normal and healthy. Kids of divorce just do it sooner. And, my friend counseled, it's very gratifying as those new relationships develop and flourish. For over time, kids reflect on their parents' divorce as we all reflect back on our lives, and if you acted well, and treated your ex with kindness, your post-divorce relationship with your kids will be so sweetened by that.

That's what it's all about, right? Being the best parent we can be? Doing what's best for the kids?

⬌

Further reading on studies of divorce and kids:

Is Divorce Bad For Children?
Scientific American
https://www.scientificamerican.com/article/is-divorce-bad-for-children

The Impact of Divorce on Young Children & Adolescents
Psychology Today
https://www.psychologytoday.com/blog/surviving-your-childs-adolescence/201112/the-impact-divorce-young-children-and-adolescents

How Divorce Affects Children
Emery About Children and Divorce
http://emeryondivorce.com/how_divorce_affects_children.php

Exercise

It's playtime. Let's play "pretend." Practice dealing with two of the biggest kid issues:

Telling kids their parents are splitting up.

Custody—who lives where and when.

These are just warm ups. Don't even try to get every detail right or think of every possible thing.

Part 1: Telling the kids

How will you tell your kids about your break up? Telling our kids is one of the hardest moments in a split. But we meet the challenge better if we're prepared. Consider the whole scene carefully, ahead of time. When tell them? Where? Who says what? If more than one child, do you tell them together?

And also: What does everybody do *after* the big conversation? Best to have some plan, keep everybody occupied? Or just smile and say, ok, thanks for listening, you can go play XBox now?

What if there's a meltdown? What if the meltdown isn't a kid— it's you or your ex?

Try thinking of the whole thing as a movie script scene:

The Cast

You

What are you wearing? Are you relaxed, or faking it reasonably well? Are you sober? (*Yes* is the only ok answer.) Are you cheerful? Dark? Chatty? Silent? Are you in control of yourself or on the edge of losing it? Can you do it if it's the latter?

Your ex

Is he/she there? Sober? Cheerful? Dark? Chatty? Silent?

It's better if you two tell the kids together—present an amicable, unified front and show from the get-go, it's a breakup, not a war. But only if you both can agree to that—meaning, beforehand, you have a calm discussion about what gets said, when, and by who. And agree to *no arguing* in front of the kids. For stuff not worked out yet you both agree to tell the kids, "That's an important issue. We're still working on it. We promise, we'll talk about this again as soon as possible."

Can you do that? Maybe rehearse *that* conversation ahead of time too.

The kid(s)

If you have more than one child, can you find a time and place all can be together? If not, what sequence of separate discussions will work best? Can one child know first and keep it secret?

Are the kids going to be shocked? Or do they pretty much know there's trouble in paradise? For example, when my ex and I told our kids, they weren't exactly dumbfounded—we'd been sleeping in separate rooms a long while already.

Even though it's probably best to tell all kids together, it may be appropriate to then have individual conversations with each child afterwards. Can you and your ex do that together? Separately? Which child first? Where and when?

Anybody else

Admittedly, this is a very personal decision, but it's probably better to only have parents and kids at the initial discussion.

Having third parties present risks disrupting the intimacy and sacredness of family space. Of course, there are times where including a grandparent, therapist or even a nanny may be useful, or even necessary. Is that your situation?

Bear in mind, having third parties involved requires the advance consent not only of you and your ex but also the third party, who may not wish to play such a role, or, if they are ok attending, do not want to be taken by surprise by anything in the meeting.

The Setting

When

When will the meeting take place? How long will it last? If possible, have an open-ended time window—if the kids ask loads of questions or talk and talk, it'd be awful to have to glance at your watch and say, *Sorry honey, can we pick this up later?*

And try to meet at a "soft landing" time. Meaning, after the discussion, it's better if the kids don't have to be "on," don't have to focus on anything important—they may just need to lick their wounds. For example, meeting before the kids go to school isn't optimal. Why send kids to school with heads reeling? Likewise, do the kids have a big test the next day? Maybe it's not a great idea to break the news then send them to their rooms to study. Can the kids skip school the next day if they want?

Finally, it may seem silly but maybe it's not a great idea to meet on empty stomachs, feeling distracted or grumpy. Maybe meet over a meal? Or have cookies and fruit around?

Where

Where will you meet? In a public place? At home? In what room? At a table? On sofas? Who sits where?

And of course: Turn *off* the music, TV and games, and put phones away. *Way away.*

The Action

How does everyone gather? Do you and your ex seemingly spontaneously round up the kids? Or, given busy schedules, do you have to plan a family meeting ahead of time but somehow keep mum about the agenda?

Do you and your ex sit reasonably close together—to show, physically, it's not a war? How about body language? Can you make eye contact with your ex? Can they do so with you? Not sigh, roll eyes or look away.

When everyone's together, who speaks first? Do you and your ex each want to say a few words before letting the kids ask questions? If a kid pops out a question anyway do you and your ex ask them to be patient? Or do you just answer?

How does the meeting end? At some point the conversation probably just peters out. Then what? Do you say: *Ok well that's enough for now, we'll talk more later, now everybody can go back to what they were doing.* Or do you want to have programmed activities follow? To keep everyone a little healthily distracted after the bomb dropped? Does a younger child need special attention? From who? Both you and your ex? A babysitter or grandparent?

Should someone look in on the kids later, after the meeting? Maybe offer a smaller, quieter setting for follow on conversation? Is your ex ok with *you* doing that? Are you ok if they do it?

What will *you and your ex* do following the meeting? Kick back, have some wine and joke around? Or retreat to separate spaces to breathe and get heart rates back to normal?

Are you or your ex planning any changes immediately, as soon as the kids are in the loop? For example, will you now sleep in separate rooms? (If so, did you tell the kids so they don't have to peek around corners trying to figure out what's happening?)

What's the plan for the days and weeks immediately ahead? Have you explained *that* to the kids? (If there are to be changes in people's lives, you should explain as soon as you can.)

The Dialogue

Who says what exactly?

Can you and your ex be honest while also kind and circumspect? If Dad's pissed Mom was fooling around, or if Mom's freaked at Dad about money, can such things be put aside for the moment?

If not, can the meeting even take place? Or does each of you need to have their own separate kids meeting? Who goes first?

If you or your ex has a breakdown, is the other ok to take the high road and put the meeting and the kids ahead of any hurt feelings or anger? To calmly say something like, *Well, Mom is emotional about all this and so am I and who can blame us? But that's an issue we'll deal with later, when we can.*

Are you prepared to answer the questions most kids ask immediately: *Who's living where and when? When's all this happening? Am I still going to the same school? What's happening to our house? What's happening to our pets?*

<h>

Part 2: Custody

Initial discussions of custody and parenting plans often involve ratios—the kids are with him 50%, her 50%. Or whatever. But the actual schedule needs to be *specific*. What does 50/50 mean, exactly? The kids switch residences every day? That's a nightmare. Every month? No, long separations break hearts.

Create a rough parenting plan. Where do the kids live and when? For now, assume the best—your ex is on the same page as you. (But also know, in the real world, this may be a slog.)

Take a walk in your post-split shoes—and in your ex's. How will post-breakup life affect everyone's schedules? Will work change? Social lives *will* change—for example, you'll likely want to date again and so will your ex, so will weekends be precious?

And bake in the kids. As a legal matter, minors can't make custody demands, but in the real world, whenever possible what kids prefer should take priority.

Also, put on a soothsayer hat and predict—will today's schedule work next month? Next year? Then the next? Kids get older. Schools and activities change. Your and your ex's lives will change. Yes, you may need to create an initial parenting plan that only works for today, not the future. But it's worth giving the future a review, especially around big chunky schedule items like school vacations.

Finally, make sure to consider a dirty little secret: Single parents can, at the same time, deeply love their kids and also love the freedom of not having to be an active, hands-on parent all the time.

Ask any split parent: if you're comfortable your kids are ok, you'll really enjoy your free time. When married, you always had obligations. Paying attention to your partner. Paying attention to the kids. Now you have no spouse. And sometimes, no kids. Maybe you're a tad embarrassed to admit it but...you love it. You really love the time with no kids. Yes, you miss them terribly, can't wait for their return. You feel sad. You text and call, all the time. But you also love dropping them off. You get to be an empty-nester way before married people. For many, it's a *perk*.

To keep the schedule math simple, start with repeating, 28-day parenting plan cycles. That is, 4-week cycles which repeat:

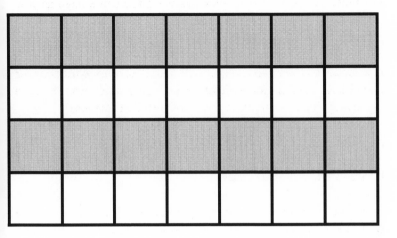

4-week cycles fit well into a 52-week year (exactly thirteen 4-week periods.) Other models can make the math complicated. For example, we can't divide a week in two because 7 days divided by 2 equals 3.5 days—and what exactly is 0.5 days?

And for now, say the split is 50/50. And let's further say that, in the 4-week diagram above, the top *row* is your week, the second is your ex's, the third is yours, and the fourth is your ex's.

But the first *column*—which day of the week should that be? That's the day when the kids switch residences. Can your and your ex's schedules allow switchover to be the same day every week? Hopefully, yes. So which day is it?

Plus, how does switchover work, exactly? What *time* does it happen? If it's a school day, do you drop the kids at school in the morning then your ex picks them up after? How does the kids stuff get moved? They shouldn't have to lug suitcases.

What if switchover is Saturday? No school. Everybody happy? Remember, that means *every* weekend is a switchover, so neither you nor your ex can easily go away for a weekend. Plus that could be a problem for kids activities.

Maybe Saturday doesn't work. Sunday evening? How late? Etc...

Here are some other practical issues:

If you live in a winter climate, how will everyone manage snow days? How about snow days that fall on a switchover day?

How will everyone manage sick days—if a kid or parent is house-bound?

How about holidays? This can be tough. One example: It's standard to say, kids with Mom on Mother's Day, Dad on Father's Day. But what if those holidays don't fall neatly in the schedule? What if Mother's Day is when the kids are with Dad? And that's an easy one. How about Christmas? What if Christmas is a big deal for *both* Mom and Dad?

Any other religious holidays to be considered? School vacations? Family events? Cousin Anna's wedding? Mom's birthday? Papa and Nana's 50th anniversary party—which is in St. Thomas?

How about unpredictable yet routine interruptions—like, say, business travel? Are both Mom and Dad willing to have simple, easy going swaps when needed? Or do you need to agree on minimum advance notice—no last minute emergencies unless it *really is* one? Or best to treat the schedule as unbreakable? If Mom needs to fly to work meetings across the country, she has to find babysitters and carpools so the kids can remain in Mom's house while she's travelling, even if Dad is just hanging at home?

Is all this making you sweat? Hyperventilate? Not surprising, it's a lot. For everyone. But that's why rehearsals like these are so worthwhile. Mulling over all this ahead of time will save you so much stress later on (not to mention legal bills).

Timing

No one here gets out alive.
—Jim Morrison

Yeah, I'm unhappy. I want to break up and just move on already. But it's just not the right timing.

Hasn't most everyone in bad relationships said those words?

Well, we're all full of bull. There is no "right timing."

If you need to find the right moment to leave, you'll probably stay in your unhappy relationship forever.

◂◈▸

Do you think it's better to stay in your bad relationship because your life's a mess and dealing with that has to come first?

Or your life's not such a mess, but there are lots of other people affected and splitting now wouldn't be fair to them.

Or it's just a complicated time now, a bad fit for a disruption.

Or you need to wait until you have your master plan, a roadmap for what to do with your life.

Or best to wait until financial things change. Or kids are older. Or you finally catch your partner, red-handed, doing whatever.

Or because, yeah, it's pretty awful now, and has been for a long while, but you'll be a rotten person if you don't at least wait a while longer to see if things change.

Silly human.

Rosebud.

Sorry—you don't know what that means?

It's from *Citizen Kane,* an old movie from 1941.

(The movie has zero to do with me, just a coincidence.)

It's in black and white with no explicit sex or violence, spaceships or superheroes, but still, it's one of the most famous films ever.

It opens somberly, with a rich old man in his fantastic castle of a home, alone, lying in bed staring at the ceiling, holding a snow globe—one of those souvenirs, full of water with a little scene inside that when you shake it, makes powder float like snow.

He utters one word:

Rosebud.

Then he expires. His dead hand lets go of the snow globe which shatters on the floor. And the rest of the movie follows a reporter writing the man's obituary, trying to figure out what "rosebud" means. The deceased was Charles Foster Kane, one of the most powerful, famous men ever. So *much* is known about his life. But "rosebud"? Nobody has a clue.

No, I'm not telling you what it means. (Watch the movie.) But I'll say this: Even with all his wealth, influence and power, Kane died forlorn. For the most basic, human reason. He had everything, except what he really wanted: Love. Simple, everyday love.

Yeah, yeah, yeah: *Money can't buy love.*

But the movie's much more nuanced and smart than that cliche. Kane's warm and likable. And altruistic, a tireless champion of the downtrodden and underprivileged. Very multidimensional and human, not just some oligarch whose riches can't buy love. So the movie asks: *Why* didn't Kane find love? He was a decent man who had everything and everybody. Why not *that*?

Here's my interpretation:

He wasn't honest with himself.

He could have had love if he'd looked in his heart and *admitted* that was what he wanted. And gone after it. Instead, he created a narrative in his mind, an alternative reality, where he suppressed feeling unloved and disguised the yearning as a passion to care for the average joe, an altruistic mission, receiving love from the masses, if never from the people close to him. And he's successful at that mission, and gets so caught up in that manufactured persona, he can no longer even see it *is* one. Then tough things happen, but he doesn't go for the love and help of the people close to him, who would gladly give it. Instead he feels victimized, sorry for himself, angry at the world. And in that distraction, he loses the people close to him, and loses sight that his feeling of being helpless against fate is just a mental jail cell that's actually unlocked, he can be free any time, just move on and go live his life. But he doesn't. He broods. And stays put.

Until the very end. When, alone on his deathbed, finally he's free to explore his heart, his yearning and his mistakes and— ironically, given his wealth and success—his wasted life.

Rosebud.

(No, I'm still not telling you what that means.)

Charles Foster Kane suffered a common affliction, I think. Where our natural discomfort dealing with our loneliness and yearning for love makes us comfort ourselves with a story, some alternative narrative about anything and everything except what we really feel. It's so understandable that we do that. We feel vulnerable and afraid so we use coping mechanisms, even full blown distractions, to change the channel.

But I think it's essential that we pinch ourselves from time to time. Life's not preordained. The tales of our lives have not yet been told. No one's a prisoner of fate. We have free will, we can make choices, and take actions, and start again, and again, reinvent ourselves, get a second chance—and a third and a fourth and a fifth. But it's up to *us* to make that happen. Our fairy godmother is indisposed.

As a very wise man (my late Dad) liked to say, *There are two kinds of people. Those who let things happen. And those who make things happen.*

Make things happen.

I know, life gets in the way. In the past you had more freedom to look for love and thrills, but now there's so much to deal with. You're not a kid anymore, you have responsibilities. You just don't know if you have the time and energy to start over. You don't know if you can take another heartbreak, another bad break. At least you have what you have. Maybe it's not that fulfilling but it's "the devil you know." A new life could be *worse*. Better to wait. Find the right time. When the planets are aligned. Or whatever.

But there is no right time, no perfect moment. So the right time might as well be now.

What can I say? I'm an optimist. And I will optimistically point out the big good news: *You're still breathing.* You're alive. That's either a miracle, or a completely random accident, but either way it's rare. And a gift, a blessing. Anything can happen.

The pessimistic news is, we'll all be dead someday.

But not today.

Rosebud.

Another old, pop culture nugget: *A Christmas Carol*. The Charles Dickens classic. Angels visit Scrooge and shows him his past and future. And given that special chance to reflect, Scrooge changes.

Boom!

I'm no angel but I can show *you* your future. You're in a bed. Lots of pillows. Comfortable. Oh what's that? Some stiff, crinkly plastic fitted sheet underneath. Ah, you're in a hospital. You're very old and weak. And people often soil themselves as they expire. Yeah, it's your deathbed. You feel exhausted. Drained. All the time. But still, your mind is still sharp. So you lie there, try to gather your strength. Somebody will come soon to chat, a nurse or family member or friend. That'll be nice. But it's so tiring. So until then, just rest. Yeah.

But then, as it does, your mind wanders. Reflects.

So: Did that future you stay in your discontented relationship? Have more or less the same life as you do now, for many more years?

Or did you leave? Somehow someday went off to try to find a new life. And succeeded, partly. And failed, partly. Life! Ups and downs.

Whatever you decided, is the future you happy with that choice, lying there at the end? Does the future you feel your life was a reasonably good use of your short time on Earth? (Even if you're 90, your life will feel—*will be*—short.)

And that future you—if you *stayed*, how long did that end up being? Today, in the present, you're what, 35 years old? 40? 50? On your deathbed, you're 80. Or 90. That's 30, 40, even 50 years from now. Did you spend a lot of that time wondering what life might be like if you did start fresh? Was there a point where you just gave up? Abandoned even the thought of starting anew?

Life is short. Don't waste yours.

I know, that's the most trite, maudlin, commonplace learning ever. But it's that *obvious* because it's that *true*.

No matter who we are *today*, when we're lying on our deathbeds, I think it'll be clear that whatever our traditions and cultures drilled into us about the "sanctity" of marriage or lifelong commitment, and the importance of taking into consideration other people and things when deciding about staying or breaking up, is all, just, well, bunk.

Marriage is wonderful, essential, critical for human societies to create stable platforms, nuclear families. *I'm wildly in favor of marriage.* But I'm wildly *against* the "til death do us part," part. It's just, way, way, way too much to expect from modern people. Staying in or exiting a marriage or relationship is a deeply personal decision, 99% about the individual making it. (The other 1% is about the law.) It's not selfless to be miserable, and make other people around you miserable by that state of affairs. And it's your one life. In the end, who or what else gets to make such huge decisions for us, other than ourselves?

Almost all of us pick a life partner, and get married or commit to a longterm relationship, when it *feels* right emotionally to *us*, as a very individual and personal decision, not because of what anyone else thinks, or because it's some particular time or circumstance. And we recoil at the thought of doing it any other way, right?

So why do we think that's a questionable way to decide to *end* such a relationship?

⟨⏸⟩

A word on religion:

Do I believe in God? Yes and no. I was born Jewish and celebrate that. So yes. But rationally, no. Still, I *feel* all life is connected somehow. Is that God? I don't know. But I *do* know, that's up to *me* to decide. In modernity, we can have our own individual ideas about spirituality. So if someone feels traditional religion is a big factor in relationships, I respect that. That's their decision.

But I think it's possible to reconcile traditional religion with my belief that everyone has the right to decide for themselves, on a completely selfish, "me" basis, whether to stay or break up.

Again, you're on your deathbed. Soon you'll *know*. If God exists. If there's life after death. Or just nothingness. But say it's the former. God exists. There's life after death. At death, we're judged. Does God punish souls *just* for exiting an unhappy marriage? If that's all it takes, then hell is *crowded*. And heaven pretty empty. And it's amazing huge swaths of Europe and the USA aren't pillars of salt. And I guess ancient Rome, Egypt, Greece and the like sent zero people to heaven—so many early societies didn't view divorce as a big deal.

Or maybe God doesn't judge solely on such things. And if you believe you're at essence a good person who most always tries to do the right thing, won't that count most? God is compassion and love, right? And *knows* a person's heart. If you leave a marriage for good honest reasons—and being miserable, and knowing your partner isn't happy either, is a *great* good honest reason—then won't you still be in good shape at the Pearly Gates?

<HR>

I'll close on an up note, and another cliche:

The most precious commodity is indeed time.

But lucky you, you've got it.

You're *not* on your deathbed yet.

That's a long way off, hopefully.

And while it's unlikely we'll lie on our deathbeds with *zero* regrets, it's very possible to *not* end up like Charles Foster Kane, wishing we'd had the sense to trust our hearts more, and not kid ourselves, and use our lives to pursue happiness and loving relationships. Just, don't make the mistakes Kane made. Worry about finding contentment, *not* about finding the right moment.

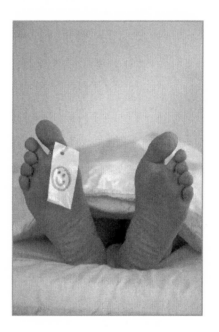

Exercise

Write your own eulogy. The short speech that the you of today will give someday many years from now at the funeral of the future you.

Two versions:

1. **You stay in your unhappy relationship.**
2. **One way or another, you breakup.**

In both versions you live to be the same age, let's say 85.

In both, you die of natural causes.

In both, you do not win the lottery or go bankrupt.

Your eulogy can be long but needn't be—Abraham Lincoln's Gettysburg Address is only 272 words, or roughly one double-spaced typed page.

Extra Credit

Watch the movie *Citizen Kane*.

Escape velocity

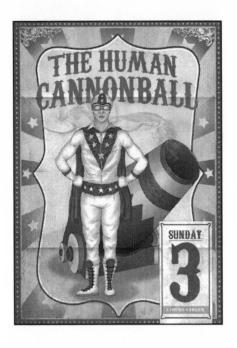

The U. S. Constitution doesn't guarantee happiness, only the pursuit of it. You have to catch up with it yourself.

—Ben Franklin

In another segment, I ask you to bake a little science—statistics—into your thinking about relationships. Well, here I go again, this time with a concept from physics: *escape velocity*. According to NASA, escape velocity is "the speed needed for an object to break away from the gravitational pull of a planet or moon." Meaning, for something to escape a planet's gravity, it must achieve a certain velocity. Or else it falls back to the planet.

Yes, this *is* rocket science. But it's simple. You've experienced it many times. Throw a ball as high as you can. Does it leave Earth and travel to the stars? No, it gets to some height then falls back. No escape velocity. Gravity wins.

My work is trying to help you achieve *relationship* escape velocity. How am I doing? Got the emotional and psychic velocity to escape the massive gravitational pull of a longterm relationship?

Don't worry if your muscles are quivering. Relationship gravity is powered by thousands of years of traditions, societal pressures and cultural stigmas. And by the normal human feelings of loyalty, commitment, devotion and love, as well as fear, sadness, inertia, and complacency. It takes a *ton* of inner strength to achieve relationship escape velocity. Even in the most obvious cases, where a relationship is lifeless or just plain awful, it still takes mighty spiritual engines to get free.

I mean, that day, way back when, when you said, *I do*—I assume you meant it? And that you were in love? Content, even eager, to settle down, for life, with that wonderful human standing next to you? Me too! And I hope you felt *joy* that day, one of the few truly blissful days of any life. And I reckon you felt relief as well: *Phew. The scary search is over! Bye-bye insecurity and loneliness. I'm not just a person anymore, I'm that celebrated pinnacle of civilization: a couple.*

Of course you're still pulled hard by that day, those feelings. We all are. It never stops. *And that's a good thing.* Even after a breakup and you're on your merry way in a new life, you'll still cherish that day. *It was a great day.* Maybe, when the dust has really settled, you'll even deeply cherish your marriage or relationship, despite that it didn't last forever.

I do.

But now it's, well, *now*. Not then. That gravitational pull is from the past, not from the place where it can do you the most good—from the future. Aim your rocket there, to the stars.

And that "til death do us part" thing. Is that still exerting strong pull?

Til *death*? Really, for real? *Death*?

Holy moley, hopefully that's such a long time from now, isn't it? Are five words going to constrain your entire, one life, no matter what? Five little words get to corral you into, what? Five decades of discontent?

*Yeah, I know. But I can't face feeling I was dumb. I can't handle people knowing I made such a big mistake. It's humiliating. And I just can't deal with being alone again. I just **can't**.*

Of course. I get it. We all get it. Such are the voices in your head. The raging debate in *all of our heads*.

Well. Sorry but maybe it's time to take sides. One of those voices has to win: Fall back to the planet. Or rocket free.

You know where I stand:

People in unhappy relationships should break up if they feel it's best. That's a normal, healthy response to an unfortunate situation. No one should feel guilty or pressured to suffer. For many, "til death do us part" is not a reasonable oath. Today's lives are too long—*and too short*—to expect life partnerships to be happy and functional forever.

Who decreed we should beat ourselves up and stay mired in misery just because we didn't win the lottery?

In rocket science, a key factor in escape velocity is *fuel*. Energy. Objects move or get moved by some engine, which consumes fuel. A critical issue then is, does the rocket have enough?

I hope you know: I firmly believe *you* do.

You see it every time your stomach flips thinking about your situation. It takes a lot of energy to flip a human stomach.

You see it every time you pound the steering wheel in frustration over something. Ask the steering wheel.

You see it when you find yourself sobbing at some movie way more than it deserves—because that show made a crack in the fuel tank in your heart and all that pent-up energy gushed out.

Which is all good news. You're not dead yet. You're very much alive. *Loaded* with life energy, fuel to achieve escape velocity.

◄ll►

> *Grant me the serenity to accept the things I*
> *cannot change*
> *Courage to change the things I can;*
> *And wisdom to know the difference.*
> Reinhold Niebuhr, *The Serenity Prayer*

The famous *Serenity Prayer* is core to AA and other 12-step programs, for good reason. It's simple, clear, brilliant counsel.

Maybe you can use it to turbo charge your rocket. I'm not saying you're some kind of addict, or relationship coaching is akin to substance counseling. I'm no expert in those things. But I am saying that, like people in 12-step programs, folks dealing with unhappy relationships are *starting over*. So maybe *The Serenity Prayer* can help you navigate your rocket, pointed away from what you can't change, and towards what you can. And to keep on course, trying, always always trying, to know the difference.

⟨‖⟩

In any case, hopefully now at least you're feeling a bit wizened, a little more clear. You know: You're not alone. You've done nothing wrong. You can have a new life if you want. And that while breaking up is always a big challenge with risks and tough times, it's not a zero sum game—a person moving on need *not* hurt others. We can forgive. No matter what. Even ourselves.

And nothing is forever.

Except death.

Which *is* forever.

I know you're scared of being alone. Who blames you? But may I gently suggest: Perhaps you are, in fact, right now, already alone? And alone in a place you can't even be by yourself. Spiritual, emotional, sexual isolation... yet joined to another person you don't really want to be with. And who probably doesn't really want to be with you. Would actually *being* alone be worse?

So. I've deployed thousands of words now, trying to nudge you to forgive yourself, forgive everyone else, process and embrace that you have only one life, and that unhappy relationships can and should end, and starting over is a huge amount of work and risk, but the alternative is probably worse. There's only one place left to go. My Nana Hilda.

Now in her late 90's, my Nana Hilda is what a less sensitive time might have called a tough broad. She was an unlikely relationship coach. She's my Nana. We're close, but not confidantes. She's supportive and loving but doesn't win awards for delicacy—she had a hardscrabble youth on the unpaved streets of Kiev in the Ukraine, or whatever it was called back then, and still has that caustic, survivor veneer. And she has no experience of divorce—she enjoyed a loving, 50+ year marriage until my grandfather passed away.

My breakup was barely two days old when she called. I was surprised—the situation was so new, I wasn't sure what she (or anybody) knew. My ex and I had told almost no one and were still living together. But Nana Hilda butted right in:

"So I heard. Come talk. Tomorrow."

That's my Nana Hilda. She summons people. And when you're that age, people come. I met her at a local coffee place. Fragile of body but firm of mind, she offered no platitudes. As soon as my butt hit the chair, she looked me in the eye and said, *Listen: It's for the best. Just get the heck out. And get everything done fast.*

Well!

Oh? I said, buying time. I was a bit surprised to hear that from a person a) of traditional values who I assumed was no fan of divorce, and b) I knew was deeply fond of my soon-to-be-ex.

Look, Nana Hilda said, putting down her cup with purpose, *When I was growing up, my parents didn't even like each other. It was obvious. But in those days nobody had a choice. They stayed together. And it was awful. For everybody. But you don't have to do that. Go enjoy your life. Now, while you can. Both of you.*

And that was that. She sipped her coffee and leaned back, eyes on mine. I said I was grateful for her candor and advice. I didn't offer details about anything and she didn't ask for any, just asked if my kids were OK, twice, and I said, yes, twice, and she told me, twice, to *not* drag them into it. Then we chatted about where I was thinking of moving, was I ready to date, that sort of thing.

God bless her. Pitch perfect coaching, in just minutes, for the price of coffee and a muffin:

Go enjoy your life.

Now, while you can.

Both of you.

Exercise

Imagine your actual breakup. The scene where you, your partner or both of you say: It's over. And in that moment, it really is.

Write it as a movie script. Three scenes:

Scene 1: You're the decider.

You break the news to your partner. When and where will you do it? What will you say? How will they react? Will it be a long and deep conversation? Or a perfunctory one? Will nerves and emotions be raw? Or will you and your partner be controlled?

Are there other people involved? Will you need help setting up the encounter? Who will provide that help?

Are kids involved? How are they to be managed (during that particular moment and scene)? Are they elsewhere? Where?

And what will you both do immediately following the big moment and conversation? For the next hour. The next day. The next few days. Just go back to normal routines?

Scene 2: You're *not* the decider.

Imagine your partner drops the news on you. If you feel estranged and unhappy there's a good chance your partner does, too. So there may be a bombshell headed your way.

What if ten minutes from now you take a break and head to the kitchen for some tea, and your partner is standing there, awkwardly, not making eye contact, and suddenly blurts out, "It's over. We have to break up."

How do you feel? Pissed off? Shocked? Devastated? Panicked?

Relieved?

No matter how kind a person behaves in such big moments, the other person still may feel poorly treated. Which could be your partner. Or it could be you. It may just be the adrenaline of the moment. Or it may be genuine hurt and shock. When waves of emotion are washing over you will you be able to stay level headed and talk? Or will you fall apart and have to run out?

So back to the first scene for a minute: Ask yourself, when I break up with my partner, will they be able to forgive me for that very act? On the spot? Or even quickly? If not, do I care?

More importantly, when the moment is upon you two, will *you* be able to forgive? Whatever needs forgiving? Will you have the presence of mind to say to yourself: I have escape velocity. I need to be careful of hurting anyone with my rocket nozzle.

Scene 3: Two years later.

For this, your final segment Exercise, try to imagine what it will be like to have a conversation about your marriage and life together—or about anything—with your partner, a full two years after you two had the big conversation about breaking up.

Odds are, your divorce is done. Long over. There may still be some touchy feelings, but probably few. Whatever issues needed to be sorted out, have been. Including kids and money. You've moved on. And so has your partner.

Sorry, I mean, your *ex*.

You're in a new life now. The break up almost feels like ancient history. Maybe you're dating. Maybe so is your ex. Maybe one or both of you have a new serious love interest. One way or another, you now have new issues and problems, many of which have zero to do with your your ex. Who is still part of your life but in a distant way. Not uncomfortable, just not close. Maybe not friends but friendly. You have all sorts of important stuff in your life that your ex doesn't even know about. And honestly, doesn't care about. And ditto, going the other way.

So now. Be honest:

How does that feel?

Extra Credit

If you're married, look online and find the legal papers a person needs to file for divorce in your state.

Marvel at how short and simple they are.

So now what

Action is the antidote to despair.
—Joan Baez

So now what

You don't learn to walk by following rules. You learn by doing and by falling over.
　　　　　　　　—Richard Branson

Some people die at 25 and aren't buried until 75.
　　　　　　　　—Ben Franklin

Everybody holds still. Nobody gets hurt.
　　　　　　　　—Grace Jones

Be your own light.
　　　　　　　　—The Buddha

I have a bias for action. It's just part of who I am. I believe it's usually better to do *something* rather than nothing.

So now what?

Do something.

Maybe that something is a divorce or breakup. But maybe it's something else. Something smaller, more incremental. But still: Do something. Make some sort of change. In some fashion, don't live tomorrow the same as yesterday.

Actually, I should say, do something *else*. You've already done something big: You did this program. So don't stop, do something else. Did you do all the Exercises here? Or did you skip some because they seemed too hard? Well, do the Exercises.

But beyond this program, maybe just do something small. Break some relationship pattern or habit that bugs you. Try a new sex position. Stop drinking alcohol for a while.

Or maybe do something bigger. Like, f*** it, get a divorce?

The final Exercise, following this segment, has a long list of small, incremental things you can do, relationship-related and otherwise, to keep your mind and body fresh, and keep your own bias for action alive and kicking. But no matter what, just don't do nothing. Don't just retreat back into your unhappy situation. Find some way, and then another, and then another, to not feel stuck, or powerless, or complacent, or paralyzed. Don't give up. Do something. Every night, aim to go to bed thinking, *Ok, I took yet another tiny step today. I didn't give up. I didn't close my eyes to my situation. Someday I will have a better life. Much better. It's a huge mountain to climb but today I took one more step.*

And say "yes" to mistakes, to screwing things up. You will, and so what. When you fall down, get up. And do something else. And don't forget: Forgive yourself. Yes, you mucked things up all sorts of ways, and all along the way. But so what. We all did. For most of us, much of the time life can really suck. But living is too short for self pity. Most important, being in an unhappy relationship is not a sin. It's not a mistake. Stuff happens, to everyone. You started your relationship with good feelings and intentions. So did your partner. Things changed for the worse. People made poor decisions, did regrettable things, said harsh words. Such are normal human events. And what's done is done. Thinking about leaving the relationship is not a sin. Actually leaving it isn't either, if that's what's right for you. The only sin, in my opinion, is doing nothing.

As my late Dad liked to say, *There are two kinds of people. Those that let things happen. And those that make things happen.* Make things happen. Sometime the results are horrible. But always there's a huge feeling of satisfaction: You're in the game. You're not a bystander in your own life. That, in and of itself, is a rewarding form of success. That alone makes life better. Even in failure there's satisfaction and pride in being able to say:

F*** it, I'm doing something.

In any moment of decision, the best thing you can do is the right thing, the next best thing is the wrong thing, and the worst thing you can do is nothing.

—Theodore Roosevelt

Exercise

Ready to *do something?*

Time to de-rut. I first heard about this type of exercise in the movie, *My Dinner With Andre.* And I've been doing it myself ever since. It's a big, ongoing exercise, but done as many small actions, done in any order and whenever you like, all at once or anytime.

The big idea is, you're in a rut. Actually a lot of them. And it's healthy to get out of ruts, right? And avoid them in the future. How? By *doing something* about them, by taking deliberate actions to see and break out of your ingrained behavior patterns. All through our lives we develop habits we're not even aware of. Hundreds of them. Even the best of us sleepwalk through life in some ways. Navigate on autopilot. And that lulls us into complacency. In a de-rut, we force ourselves to notice and undo habits, wake up and keep bodies and minds fresh.

Sound complicated? It's not. Here's an example:

Do you always brush your teeth with the same hand? I'll bet you've been repeating the exact same teeth brushing sequence and motions for many years. Always the same. Same time. Same routine. Same motion. Same hand. You've done this, what, 400-800 times a year? For 20 years? How many tens of thousands of times have you mindlessly, numbingly, done the same thing?

That's a rut.

Does it do harm? Maybe not on the surface. Superficially, it's still doing the basic good it was intended to—brushing your teeth. Good. Don't stop. But switch hands. Break the habit. Step out of the rut. And not just one time, how about for the next month?

How about until the "new" hand feels as natural and ingrained as the "old" hand does. Then switch again. Get it?

Think about all the ruts carved deep into your life:

- Do you always shave with the same hand?
- Do you always shave your face or body in exactly the same strokes and pattern and order?
- Do you always always shave at the sink? In the shower?
- Do you always take the same route to work? To school? The market? Take another. Change it up.
- Do you always sleep on the same side of the bed?
- Do you always always sleep in the same position?
- Do you always get dressed in the same order? Underwear first, then socks then shirt etc?
- Do you always brush your teeth then floss? Floss first.
- Do you always *always* wipe your rear end with the same hand? It's not the law, you know.
- Do you always always prepare your coffee or tea the same way? Put sugar in the cup before the coffee.
- Do you always shower at the same time in your routine?
- Do you always park in one place or on one side of the garage?
- When you park, do you always back the car in or pull in forward?
- When was the last time you adjusted your car seat?
- Do you always carry your cell phone in the same place?
- Change your ringtone.
- Change your outgoing voicemail message. To something really different.
- Do you always always shop at the same supermarket? Same drugstore? Why?
- Do you always buy the same foods? Same brands?
- Do you always sit in the same seat at your kitchen counter or dining table?
- Do you always masturbate with the same hand?
- Do you always masturbate in the same way? (Good news: a world of fun awaits.)

- Do you always consume your news in the same order? This web site then that one. Sports then arts then news.
- Do you always wash your body parts in the same order, same pattern, in the bath or shower?
- Change the sound or radio station on your alarm clock alarm.
- Brush/comb your hair with the other hand.
- Use another bathroom in your house. As your go-to bathroom. Ditto, at work.
- Keep your wallet/keys in a different pocket.
- Deposit your wallet/keys in a different place when you get home.

Of course, this is just a partial list. Please contact me with ruts that should be added!

One last thing: Never stop de-rutting. We should all do these things all the time, for the rest of our lives.

Extra Credit

Watch *My Dinner With Andre*. It's a strange, wonderful movie—practically just one long scene, dinner at a restaurant with two old friends who haven't been together in a long time. It's a charming, thought-provoking meditation on what it is to be human, on life, love and the pursuit of happiness. It has one or two odd or meandering stretches but stick with it—I predict by the end you'll be moved. I've rewatched this one dozens of times. Makes me laugh a little, cry a little, and think a lot, every time.

It's on YouTube (free, as of this writing) and elsewhere.

Additional resources

The delights of self discovery are always available.
      —Gail Sheehy

Additional Resources
are also available free at
GetHappy.Life

A Divorce Dictionary

Like so many things in the modern world, divorce and the legal dissolution of relationships has its own vernacular. Here's a brief glossary of some common terms everyone should understand, at least a little bit—after all, in the legal world a small word change can often compel a big life change.

Disclaimer: I'm not an attorney, not an accountant, not a mediator, not a financial advisor. Don't use this as gospel. It's not definitive. In some cases, it may not be entirely accurate. And please don't make any big or final decisions based on this. If you need legal counsel—and most of us do—then talk to a lawyer.

In alphabetical order:

Alimony (aka Spousal Support)

The recurring payments provided by one former spouse to the other, to create better balance between their disparate individual incomes or financial circumstances. Numbers, percentages and ratios are usually open to negotiation, but also are almost always calculated, at least in part, using guidelines in the laws of the former couple's home state. For example, she's a big earner; he's a smaller one, so she owes him alimony, paid monthly (or on some agreed upon recurring schedule) for whatever number of years are proscribed in their particular state's law.

Alimony is different than, and disconnected from, any Child Support payments a splitting couple may agree on. Alimony is only to address post-breakup financial inequities, if any. Child Support is intended to help care for children only, not redress other imbalances. Ex-partners may agree on one or the other or both such payments.

Attorney

Attorney is just another word for "lawyer." Both words mean the same thing—someone who has a state-issued license to practice law, by virtue of having passed that state's Bar Exam, which is a test administered by the local Bar Association—the professional lawyers association.

Some states do not require that people have a law school degree before taking the Bar Exam; most states do. There may be reputation benefits, or human network benefits, but there are no practical or legal benefits to having gone to a big name law school or having passed the bar exam on the first try. You can fail the Bar Exam repeatedly and keep re-taking it until you pass. Scrappy lawyer Tina Tenacity, who didn't go to law school, or went to mail order law school and failed the bar exam ten times before passing, has the same rights and privileges as an attorney as does Baron Brahmin, who was editor of the Harvard Law Review and passed the bar exam in his sleep. Both are credentialed lawyers, officers of the Court. Tina may be so smart, savvy and brave she crushes Baron. Or not. So whether their paths to being lawyers matters is up to you. Do the homework: Ask for references.

Child Support

In most circumstances, when children are involved in a divorce or family break up, the law and Courts take special care to look out for the kids' interests, as a separate matter from the other terms of the split, or the circumstances of the parents. There is basically no situation where the law or a Judge will allow children to suffer to take care of anyone or anything else.

Child support is the money one parent pays the other, usually on an ongoing basis but sometimes in a lump sum, for the care and comfort of their shared children. The amount and schedule of payments is almost always regulated under law, but the two parents may agree on different terms, as long as those terms are the same or better than the law requires. No parent may trade child support for a car, for example.

Various factors go into calculating child support but the most important are:

A. Will one parent have a larger responsibility for the care and comfort of the children?

B. How much does it reasonably cost to provide decent care and comfort to the children?

C. Is decent care and comfort enough? Or has the child been brought up in a better-than-decent lifestyle that should be continued?

D. How much can the paying parent afford to pay?

E. What are the applicable, local state laws?

States have different regulations but Child Support is almost always carefully governed by law. Any decent, local attorney or mediator will know what your state proscribes, or you can look it up online. Here's a decent summary:

http://bit.ly/1scV2C7

Collaborative Attorney

This is a fairly new, modern idea—that, to avoid costly, painful litigation fought in a Courtroom, people can work with Collaborative Attorneys, to create a less antagonistic process, leading to an out-of-court settlement, all the while each splitting partner still has the benefit of personal legal counsel. (Which is unlike when a couple uses a mediator. See *Mediator*.)

Since 2009 there has been a movement to create uniform guidelines and principles for this type of thing into specific state laws. But as of this writing, while some states have adopted such laws, most have not.

For our purposes here, though, there's no need to worry about specific laws. In virtually every state you can find attorneys who bill themselves as Collaborative Attorneys, and who will try to get you that more amicable, out-of-court settlement.

Of course, your soon-to-be-ex has to agree to this framework and also hire a Collaborative Attorney. Some Collaborative Attorneys market themselves in teams—one for you, one for your soon-to-be-ex—with the selling point being, we the Collaborative Attorneys have done this before, we know each other and how this works, if the goal is speed, cost-containment and amiability, then it's a plus your Collaborative Attorney has a pre-existing relationship with your ex's Collaborative Attorney. That may or may not be true. As always, check references.

As a practical matter, if you use Collaborative Attorneys you will probably spend time in conference rooms, either all together or separately down the hall from one another, hashing out stuff in a collaborative way. When disagreements happen, you may empower the Collaborative Attorneys to go away and on their own suggest ways to break the impasse. But even then you and your soon-to-be-ex still must approve everything; in no case are you required or even advised to let Collaborative Attorneys decide things for you.

Cost-wise, Collaborative Attorneys are still attorneys and bill by the hour, but given their commitment to amiability, there should be less cost than hiring traditional, combative attorneys—it's painful how many hours get billed as antagonistic lawyers snipe at each other in endless emails, filings, phone calls and meetings. In theory, that's all eliminated with Collaborative Attorneys—as also are expensive, awful hours in courtrooms.

An important caveat: "Collaborative" may or may not mean "peaceful." In the world of Collaborative Law, there is an unfortunate subculture of "wolves in sheep's clothing"—lawyers who sell themselves as mellow collaborators but are really just looking for clients to milk by fighting all the time anyways. But on balance I think the Collaborative Law concept is a great one. It gets rid of the temptation to view divorce as a zero sum game— where there are winners and a losers, or if your ex gets something that means you lost something. It's more expensive than using a mediator, but cost is not the only factor to weigh. (See *Mediator*.)

"Common Law" Marriage

Good news: pretty much everything you think you know about so-called "common law" marriages is wrong.

Many people believe that if a couple lives together for long enough, or does certain things, then the law considers them to be married whether or not they ever actually got married or registered their union with the law (that is, went to City Hall etc.)

Not true. In the vast majority of US states, there is simply no such law or trigger. Marriage is defined as a willing lawful union of two people who have taken the appropriate legal steps, e.g. got a marriage license or certificate. No other couples are married.

A small number of states do have "common law marriage" statutes or regulations on their books, but these are rarely if ever enforced or even brought up, and they usually have very specific requirements for being invoked—say, if a couple describes themselves and acts as though married, for example by filing tax returns jointly or if one partner uses the other's last name.

All this is likely irrelevant for you but if you think it's a factor in your split, do your homework online or talk to an attorney to find out what's what in your state.

"Conflicting Out" an attorney

This is a tactic used by people who want to prevent their soon-to-be-ex from hiring a certain attorney. It's pretty much the same thing as interviewing a prospective attorney to see if you want to hire her. But then the trick is, once you've spent any time with that attorney and shared personal details of your situation, you've then wrapped "attorney client privilege" (that is, professional confidentiality) around your relationship with that particular attorney *whether or not you actually hire them.* Which means that particular attorney is now prohibited from working with your soon-to-be-ex.

The point is, if there are divorce attorneys that are known to be truly scary or impressive or who routinely scorch the earth to get their clients what they want, you may want to prevent your soon-to-be-ex from working with them against you, whether or not you personally want to hire them to be *your* lawyer. So you meet them ASAP and "conflict them out."

Some divorce attorneys are so well known for being fearsome nuclear weapons, they know they're constantly being "conflicted out," so they charge fees for initial consultations. In their view, if you're going to "conflict them out" you should pay for the privilege (which, if you think about it, is entirely consistent with the reason you want to conflict them out in the first place.) But when you call to set up your meeting, you don't have to mention "conflicting them out" (and you shouldn't.) Just ask if they charge fees for initial consultations, and their office will tell you.

Custody

If a splitting couple has children then custody of the kids must be decided in the *Divorce Agreement*. Such can be a difficult and nuanced negotiation but I'll try to summarize some key aspects.

First, keep in mind that the law and the judge always want to put the best interests of the children first. Period. And if you and your ex can't agree, the judge will decide what's best for your child. Which may not be what you want. So tread lightly. And know that while a judge is very unlikely to rewrite a deal if a divorcing couple both seem content with an agreement, the judge can and will do so if he feels the best interests of the children have not been adequately addressed.

Next, there is a popular misperception that custody is a zero sum game, where one spouse wins and the other loses. This is simply not true. The two spouses can agree on any arrangements they want, and hopefully where both feel content. I think this always should be the goal. There is no requirement that either parent be given "primary" custody, or any dominant role. The two parents can agree that custody is 50/50 and that neither can unilaterally rule. In my own Divorce Agreement the entire custody issue is covered in just one sentence: "The Husband and Wife shall have shared legal custody of the children."

All the logistical details and everything else—and there typically is much, much else—is usually called the Parenting Plan. This covers the many practical parenting issues that also usually get negotiated. Although custody is covered by one sentence in my divorce agreement, the Parenting Plan takes up several pages detailing various day in day out, year in year out, practical issues, for example, how school vacations get divided up.

But if one divorcing parent does get "primary" custody, then that parent is the decider if they choose to be. They can always solicit the opinion of their ex, but they're not obligated to do so. This does not mean that the primary custody parent can just impose their will without restraint. The non-primary parent can always sue and ask a judge to decide. And the judge will almost always make their ruling based on what he believes is the best interests of the children, regardless of what either parent says.

In any case, the goal of any custody deal is to try to avoid conflicts, not create them. To create a practical framework for a relationship between the two divorced co-parents that makes life workable while keeping the children's best interests in mind. And most issues are practical, caretaking ones. Where do the children live, and when and how often? Where do they go to school? What if any medical situations need to be dealt with and when? How are holidays and vacations allocated? Who pays for school tuitions or summer camps or other child-specific expenses? Etc.

Divorce Agreement (Separation Agreement)

When you get married it's a contractual relationship, meaning it's governed by contract (and other) law. So to divorce, you need a new contract—a Divorce Agreement, aka a Separation Agreement.

This is true in every state—as is the requirement that your Divorce Agreement be approved by a judge. You do not need a lawyer to do a Divorce Agreement, you can do one yourself, or work with a mediator (which is different than a lawyer; see *Mediator*,) but you always need to get it approved by a judge.

Separation Agreements can be one page long or a thousand. They can cover just the minimum the law requires or the most arbitrary or bizarre details, say, what color underwear your kids wear on what days.

If the two divorcing people have agreed to sign their Divorce Agreement, a judge will usually approve it. With a few important caveats: The judge will want to determine—sometimes by asking, to your face, in the courtroom—that both parties understand the specifics of their Agreement, that they had ample opportunity to negotiate and think about it, and that they are signing under their own free will (meaning, they are not feeling undue pressure).

Once a judge approves it, a Divorce Agreement governs the post-marriage relationship of the two parties more or less forever. Of course, over the long course of time the Divorce Agreement may become moot, as its requirements expire or the parties move completely into their new, separate lives. But, for as long as there are obligations or disputes between the parties, the Divorce Agreement rules. If there's a dispute not covered in the Agreement, it's either worked out between the parties, or someone sues, goes into court and a judge decides. And that new agreement between the parties, or that judicial ruling, becomes part of the Divorce Agreement.

Note: Because Divorce Agreements are filed with the court, they are public documents. Meaning, anyone can see them. This is how TMZ, the National Enquirer and other gossip outlets get to publish the specifics of celebrity divorces—they go to the courthouse where the celebrity divorce was filed and get a copy of the Divorce Agreement. Does it matter that *your* Divorce Agreement is public? You may not be worried about TMZ, but how about your friends, and kids? You can be comforted that most courthouse records are not on the internet and won't be for some time. (There's way too much cost and work to digitize every court's records.) Still, given enough time everything ends up on the internet. Maybe the takeaway is, don't put anything in your Divorce Agreement you don't want anyone to ever see.

Divorce Coach

If you know what a Life Coach is, you pretty much know what a Divorce Coach is—it's a Life Coach with a specific, narrow specialty, helping people who are working or struggling through, or just thinking about, a divorce. Many coaches are formally trained and certified, though no broadly agreed upon education standards yet exist for Coaching, and there is no law, regulation or professional association (e.g. like the Bar Association for lawyers) that even requires any certification at all. So do your homework. And bear in mind, like any Coach, a Divorce Coach is not a therapist or psychiatrist. Divorce coaching is a flexible, goal-oriented process designed to support, motivate, and guide people going through divorce to help them make the best possible decisions for their future, based on their particular interests, needs, and concerns.

Divorce Papers

As divorce is a lawsuit, a form of litigation (see *Litigation*) at some point the divorcing parties have to file appropriate paperwork with a court, typically in the town or county in which the couple reside. These filings, or "Divorce Papers" are almost always very short, simple forms.

To get a divorce started, only one spouse has to file papers. In many cases, because they have together decided to get a divorce, both partners choose to file together, at the same time. But if one party chooses to file papers on their own, at some point the other spouse needs to be informed of that, and given copies of the papers. At which point they then are required to file their own set of papers, telling the court they are aware that the lawsuit (the divorce) has been inaugurated and so the legal process may begin in earnest. Different states have different schedule or calendar requirements for how much time is allowed for these type filings.

Despite what you may have seen in old movies, in almost all states, there's no need to hire a detective or marshall to "serve" divorce papers on a spouse. Probably, you can simply hand them to him or her. (To find out your state's requirements, if any, just look it up online.) Of course, if your spouse goes into some kind of weird psychological place, and denies you ever did give them the papers, well then yes, in that case, you do need to hire a process server to "serve" the papers again, and file an affidavit with the court stating that your spouse indeed has been served the papers. But that's rare—all that weird spouse has done is to buy themselves a little time, and incurred the cost of a process server (of which they'll have to pay half, of course.)

Typically when filing divorce papers you have to pay some relatively small filing fees, maybe a few hundred dollars. If you're working with an attorney, they can and should do these filings for you. If you want to save money, look online and find out what court you need to file in, and print out or download the forms and do everything yourself.

Family Property
(aka Marital Property, Assets & Debts)

In a divorce or legal split, a big issue is, who gets what? Things which are jointly owned by both splitting partners are called "family property," "marital assets" or "marital property." Couples also may have "family liabilities" or "marital debts." That is, two people in a marriage or civil union may not only jointly own possessions and wealth, they may also have obligations, debts and loans together. Which also need to be divided.

States have varying laws on how things can be sorted out, but in general, the law assumes most things are family property. A big exception is, if the two partners have specifically, already agreed that some assets or debts do *not* belong to both. That is, if a couple has a "pre-nuptial" or "post-nuptial" agreement—a formal contract they negotiated in the past (not as part of their breakup) that sets out how things get divided in the event of a split—then those pre-existing contracts rule. (See *Pre-Nuptial Agreement* and *Post-Nuptial Agreement*.) Of course, if one party claims their post- or pre-nuptial agreement should be considered invalid (say, because they were pressured to sign under duress,) then the parties either need to throw out their previous agreements and start over and renegotiate everything, or go to court and ask a judge to decide.

But the law usually does not impose itself on people; two people can agree to divide things however they want, as long as both state they are doing so informed of their rights and of their free will. And in general the law does not carve out anything—as stated above, unless the parties agree that an asset or a debt does *not* belong to both, then the law assumes it *does*, from the most valuable things—the house, mortgage, business, cars, pets, family photos, retirement accounts, etc—to the smallest—food in the kitchen cabinets, the $100 you loaned your best friend, the paper-mache cat (or whatever that is) your kid made in art class. And depending on circumstances, family property can be anything and everything, regardless of how or when stuff was acquired. Say, husband bought a valuable antique car well before he was married. But now, divorcing, many years have passed and the couple have no pre- or post-nuptial agreements, so the car is now a marital asset and the wife is entitled to half its value. (Since you can't cut a car in half, they either sell it or get it appraised and the husband pays the wife 50% of its value, either in cash or with something else she agrees to take.)

In some places and cases, the duration of a marriage can play a role in determining what is family property. (See *Long Term versus Short Term Marriages*.)

Future Income

In a divorce or legal breakup, naturally, a couple's *existing* shared property and debts get divided up one way or another. But the law also may allow for, or even require that, the parties divide up *future* property, income and debts.

For example, say a wife worked to help pay for her husband's medical school. A judge could agree he owes her for that, either to reimburse her for the medical school cost, or also to give her some part, maybe even as much as half, of the ongoing and *future* financial benefit of his being a doctor. That is, of his professional income. But maybe the wife only paid for part of the husband's medical school costs and the husband has student loans. So the judge also requires that the wife help pay off the loans. Or some other blended formula. Maybe the judge imposes, or the parties agree to, some kind of limits on the deal. For example, maybe the wife only gets a certain amount of money, or only gets a percentage of his income, for a certain number of years.

It can be complicated. Another example:

Commonly, two spouses exist in their marriage in one household where their two incomes (from all sources) are pooled to cover expenses. With the divorce, they're breaking into two new households. One new household has her income. One has his. Maybe she earns $200,000/year but he earns $50,000 year. They've agreed on how to divide up their possessions and debts, but is he entitled to some of her income in the future? Could be. The usual rationale is, they both are entitled to continue living more or less the same lifestyles as before the divorce, or if that's not possible, then neither should have their lifestyle reduced that much more than the other. So a judge may rule the husband is entitled to some of her future income. Since as a married couple they had $250,000 combined annual income, maybe after the divorce they both get $125,000 per year each, which means she owes him $75,000 per year. Or some other formula. Local state law may have an effect, too, for example, defining the number of years the wife can be required to pay her ex-husband that way. In any case, often the law allows people to negotiate not just the division of their present circumstances, but also future ones.

Lifestyle

A general term, used to describe the basic financial situation and level of material comforts of an individual, group or family. Divorcing people often try to maintain their married "lifestyle" — the level of comfort to which they were accustomed in the marriage. This can be a big deal if the divorce could leave one partner significantly wealthier than the other. On the other hand, if a divorce requires that both partners reduce their lifestyles relatively equally, there's nothing to be done. On the other, other hand, if a couple is super-wealthy but after the divorce he's still going to be super-wealthy but she's only going to be wealthy, she can argue she needs a particular financial settlement to maintain her super-wealthy lifestyle, or to allow their children to maintain their super-wealthy lifestyle that, on her own, she can't afford.

For example, say Dad is CEO of a huge business. Mom is a school teacher. Both are hardworking, honorable people. Dad is going to pay Mom very generous alimony (see *Alimony*.) No problem. But how much child support? Just enough to cover the basics? Food, clothing, health care, schools, occasional vacations? Before the divorce the children had nannies and cooks and flew first class, etc. Mom argues the children should not be deprived of that lifestyle despite that her teacher salary plus the alimony can't provide it. Dad disagrees; he feels he's paying plenty already. But Mom persists, they end up in court, the judge agrees with Mom and orders Dad's child support payments to be ten times higher. Dad hates it but unless he wants to be in contempt of court, he pays. An extreme example, but get it?

Litigation

This is just another word for lawsuit, the legal dispute-resolution process where people or parties go to court to settle a disagreement.

Marriage is a legal contract. A marriage is terminated—that is, a divorce is granted—when the spouses agree to replace their existing contract with a new one, called the Divorce Agreement. (See *Divorce Agreement*.) This almost always involves some sort of litigation—even if both spouses are the sweetest people who agree easily on everything, their Divorce Agreement must be reviewed and approved by a judge.

Some non-marriage relationships are legal contracts, e.g. "common law" marriages (see *Common Law Marriages*,) and their end also usually involves a contract and a judge—meaning, litigation.

Some relationships aren't legal contracts themselves but have elements that are contracts—for example, if two never-married lovers buy a house together, if they later break up and can't resolve the house ownership they may end up in litigation.

Long Term versus Short Term Marriages

Specifics vary by state, but the duration of a marriage can affect the financial and other settlement terms of a divorce. In a nutshell, in a short marriage, the spouses are presumed to have less close and deep ties than in a longer one. So, for example, a wife may argue that because the marriage was so short, some amount of money that belonged to her prior to getting married should not be now considered marital property, belonging to both of them (see *Marital Property*.) If the law allows and the judge agrees, that would mean she gets to keep all that particular money herself and not divide it up. Conversely, if that couple was married for a long time, then the fact that certain money belonged to the wife before the marriage will not be taken into account and it will all get divided.

The duration of a marriage may also factor into calculations about alimony, future income and other financial matters. But when it comes to custody and child support, the overriding concern is the best interests of the children. (See *Child Support.*) So regardless of a marriage duration, if splitting parents are fighting over where and when the child will live and a judge has to weigh in, then who can provide the best home and environment for the child will be the judge's primary concern, much more than some math equation that takes into account marriage duration. Likewise, in the big picture, child support calculations do not depend on how long a child's parents were together—they first and foremost depend on how much it's reasonable to assume it will cost to provide care and comfort to the child and how much each parent can afford on their own.

States have various thresholds for short versus medium versus long term marriages. Some states have three categories, for example, 0-7 years; 7-17 years; and 17+ years. If you think this may matter to you, do your homework and find out if any laws or regulations apply in your state.

Mediator

A mediator is a licensed professional who acts as a facilitator, a knowledgeable but neutral "middle man," to help two parties in a divorce (or any dispute) negotiate a legal settlement. The process of getting credentialed to be a mediator varies by state.

It's important to remember that even if the mediator you hire is an attorney, that they are not your advocate. The key difference between hiring a mediator versus an attorney is that an attorney has one client. You. Or your ex. An attorney therefore is an advocate for only one side, whose professional responsibility is to protect and further the interests of their client, even if that is at the expense of the other side, or requires a biased interpretation of a law or circumstance.

A mediator works for both parties and does not take sides. A mediator's professional responsibility is to get a deal done, any deal, as long as its lawful, and to understand their state's laws enough to have that settlement be found lawful and approved by a judge.

In divorces, the upside of using a mediator is the process tends to be less expensive and faster. The mediator does not want to hear, and will push back against having to listen to, your problems. Or your ex's problems. Or complaints. Or stories. Or anything except getting a deal done, relatively quickly.

All good, right? But there's a downside risk, too. From a mediator's perspective, a divorce is basically a list of boxes that need to get checked off. Property accounted for and divided? Check. Children accounted for and custody deal in place? Check. Alimony calculated, if any? Check. When all the boxes are checked, you're done, and off the deal goes to a judge.

But it could be a bad deal. No one is looking out for, let alone protecting, your interests. That's not a mediator's job. The mediator is not looking out for either party's interests. Most mediators try to be fair, of course, but then in the end, what's fair? So the mediator focuses on just getting the deal done. And you can end up getting the minimum lawful deal, despite that you arguably deserve a better one. Or just a cleaner, simpler, or more comprehensive one.

Again, a mediator is not responsible for either, both or neither party getting a good deal, or even the right deal, as long as the parties agree to the deal and it conforms to law. If you show up to a mediator meeting high on drugs, or just in a totally weird mood, and agree to give all your money and property to your ex, leaving you penniless and unemployed, well, ok fine. That's your call. The "division of family property" box gets checked and the mediator moves on. But any half-decent lawyer representing you would never let that happen.

In a situation where the two parties just can't agree, a mediator will attempt to bridge the gap. But they're not out to win prizes for creativity. They'll start by saying, meet halfway. And if that doesn't work, they'll offer slight deviations from halfway and see who caves first. Box checked, moving on.

Finally, if you ask a mediator for an opinion, most will not give it. They'll always offer you their understanding of the law and how it applies to your deal—for example, if you have no idea what alimony is or if you're entitled to it, they'll explain your state's laws and how they may apply, given whatever the mediator knows about your situation. But if you have a lawyer, they may believe you should get more than the law allows, and pursue a strategy to fight to get that.

"No Fault" Divorce

In the past, the law required that couples could not get a divorce unless one or both was found to be "at fault"—guilty of some legal transgression that, in the eyes of a court, made the marriage unsalvageable. Otherwise, the couple had to stay married, no matter how miserable they were or how they both wanted out. And judges didn't just take a person's word that their spouse was at fault: If you sued for divorce, you needed some evidence or proof your spouse was guilty of some such offense, e.g. adultery, "mental cruelty," etc. As amply dramatized in popular culture over the years, this gave rise to a seamy industry of private detectives who acquired evidence for divorce suits.

But the really bad consequence of these antiquated divorce laws was, if a couple wanted to get a divorce just because they were tired of each other, somebody still had to be found to be at fault. It didn't matter if both husband and wife wanted out, a divorce could only be granted if someone was found guilty of some legal transgression, even if it was all just silly theatrics. So the perceived public humiliation of this "at fault" requirement kept many unhappy couples married for many unhappy years.

Thank goodness, we no longer live in those times. Judges and lawmakers no longer believe it is the court's or government's job to force any person to stay in any marriage. In the mid 20th century, various US states began creating new divorce laws, eliminating the need for somebody to be "at fault"—ergo, the name "no fault." Today nearly every state allows "no fault" divorces. No one has to be guilty of anything. No one can be forced to stay in a marriage, period. If one person in a marriage wants a divorce, their wedlock can and will be ended, period.

And despite what you may have seen in old movies, because of "no fault" laws, today the old "at fault" transgressions are technically no longer available to use to try to extract concessions in a divorce. For example, if you discover your spouse is cheating, you have every right to be enraged and get divorced, but unlike the old days you probably do not have the right to claim that your partner's infidelity means you're owed money or damages.

Of course, the liberalization of divorce laws has not changed human nature. Divorce attorneys (and all people) still try to use negative portrayals of people either to influence a judge's decisions (judges are just human, too) or attack a person to try to make them agree to things. Threats and extortion are still used, even if such bullying no longer has any real basis under law.

Pre-Nuptial Agreement

A Pre-Nuptial Agreement is a contract, negotiated and signed by two partners who plan to marry but before they actually do, that describes, often in considerable detail, what will happen if the couple divorces in the future. In short, it's an advance Divorce Agreement, in case later there's a split. ("Pre" just means the agreement has been signed before a marriage. "Nuptial" is just another word for "marriage.")

There is no legal requirement anywhere for any couple to ever have a pre-nuptial agreement. Most couples do not have one. Those that do have such agreements tend to be couples where perhaps one or both partners has been married and divorced before, and experienced things they don't want to again. Or where one or both partners have property or wealth, or businesses or deals, they want to make certain remain outside the marriage and do not become family property. (See *Family Property*.) Or where one or both partners simply has strongly held views on what certain divorce terms should be if there ever is one, and they want to get it on paper and agreed to ahead of time.

This is not to say that any couple who wants one can not have a pre-nuptial agreement. Anyone can.

Like all contracts, pre-nuptial agreements can be one page or a thousand pages long. There's no standard, it's entirely up to the couple what does or does not go into a pre-nuptial agreement.

If a couple with a pre-nuptial agreement does get divorced, it's not always certain how effective that agreement will be. Various states treat pre-nuptial agreements in various ways—in some places they are very strictly enforced, in some places less so, and in all states a divorcing spouse can go into court to say that their pre-nuptial agreement should not be enforced because of some mitigating circumstance—for example, if a spouse can claim convincingly that he or she was coerced into signing the agreement, or did not receive fair legal counsel before doing so.

Post-Nuptial Agreement

A post-nuptial agreement is exactly the same thing as a pre-nuptial agreement, except that the two partners who create and sign it are already married at the time they do.

Restraining Order

As in other situations, in a divorce process one party can ask a judge to limit another party's physical access to certain people or places or things. If the judge agrees to do this, the judge's ruling is called a Restraining Order—as the name implies, it restrains a person or persons from doing certain things or being in certain places. Most judges look very poorly on attorneys or people who come looking for restraining orders without very, very compelling grounds for seeking one. Being legitimately scared for someone's or something's safety and security is a compelling reason. Just being totally pissed off is not.

Playlists for a breakup

When going through changes, music is very important to me. Actually, it's essential all the time. Here are some playlists I think you may find soothing, hopeful, rousing, or good for fist-pounding and venting. Some lyrics are topical, spot on. Others are more subtle, more about invoking a mood. Like David Bowie's *Right*. The words are abstract but the song's mood really grabs the heart: *"Taking it all the right way... Keeping it in the back... Taking it all the right way... Never no turning back..."*

To just click and listen to these playlists and tunes—and to make suggestions of other songs we should add—visit us at GetHappy.Life

Moods

16 songs, 1 hour 8 minutes

Spotify:

https://open.spotify.com/user/12138164235/playlist/70x9zeKbj mNBQ4QzTkzahf

Soundcloud:

https://soundcloud.com/stevenkane-1/sets/moods

YouTube (playlist):

https://www.youtube.com/playlist?list=PLvwpjZgRH-TAGyDqODHDrxRH999AJJQue

YouTube (individual videos):

Tame Impala: *Be Above It*
https://youtu.be/a5u8KfHXxwg

Broken Bells: *Trap Doors*
https://youtu.be/92bZjceB-Wk

David Bowie: *Right*
https://youtu.be/Gqtp1tvpkBk

Moby: *Porcelain*
https://youtu.be/IJWlBfo5Ojo

Little Feat: *Easy To Slip*
https://youtu.be/jHKFkLhr4_I

Talking Heads: *Once in A Lifetime*
https://youtu.be/Ca-WSWaSUkk

Grace Jones: *Everybody Hold Still*
https://youtu.be/7KBgHi6oCSo

Ray Lamontagne: *Hey, No Pressure*
https://youtu.be/hQ2whG32g_o

Alabama Shakes: *Don't Wanna Fight*
https://youtu.be/x-5OX7CO26c

Ha Ha Tonka: *Lessons*
https://youtu.be/mUpdTpzaDBw

El Perro Del Mar: *Walk On By*
https://youtu.be/1PJaTQF6Dv4

Leonard Cohen: *In My Secret Life*
https://youtu.be/NW7oNpzBSGc

Blackmill: *Let It be*
https://youtu.be/sDI6HTR9arA

Tom Misch: *Crazy Dream (feat. Loyle Carner)*
https://youtu.be/Sa5HNkGrl8E

Lana Del Rey: *Lust For Life (ft. The Weeknd)*
https://youtu.be/eP4eqhWc7sI

Delerium: *Silence (feat. Sarah McLachlan)*
https://youtu.be/ZA-je1_Ejq0

F*** this

16 songs, 1 hour

Spotify:

https://open.spotify.com/user/12138164235/playlist/0EOG5nE
Y7QSs5zIEMysCdu

Soundcloud:

https://soundcloud.com/stevenkane-1/sets/f-this

YouTube (playlist):

https://www.youtube.com/playlist?list=PLvwpjZgRH-
TD2YzHlNaRFnvPoJhgol1wY

YouTube (individual videos):

The Struts: *Kiss This*
https://youtu.be/r61Xj0pHawE

Eamon: *F*** it*
https://youtu.be/QYwyaCd8MyI

Nancy Sinatra: *These Boots Are Made For Walking*
https://youtu.be/m2fPkzJsMU8

Superchunk: *Slack Motherfucker*
https://youtu.be/-c_GX2CYkcQ

Above & Beyond Present Oceanlab: *I Am What I Am*
https://youtu.be/KKyYgYq4MtE

Eminem (feat. Rhianna): *Love The Way You Lie*
https://youtu.be/uelHwf8o7_U

Robert Palmer: *What's It Take*
https://youtu.be/FaZ6Kpo51dk

Cee Lo Green: *Forget You*
https://youtu.be/bKxodgpyGec

Linkin Park & Jay Z: *Points of Authority/99 Problems*
https://youtu.be/PwzSb92YWKo

Grace Jones: *Bullshit*
https://youtu.be/KyxgvPdO5ok

Lucinda Williams: *Joy*
https://youtu.be/J8tmhcYq_3o

Elvis Presley: *Devil In Disguise*
https://youtu.be/emjLXdsj6xA

Fleetwood Mac: *Go Your Own Way*
https://youtu.be/IPBcoIlGp-8

Churchill: *Change*
https://youtu.be/Im8zYhFBoJA

The O'Jays: *Back Stabbers*
https://youtu.be/RmXRQ3vfzcA

Broken Bells: *Control*
https://youtu.be/q6azqrFDXfY

Future Islands: *Light House*
https://youtu.be/VFUZDXIRdlo

Woe is me

14 songs, 56 minutes

Spotify:

https://open.spotify.com/user/12138164235/playlist/14jyB8yo6tkw8MychWnO1X

SoundCloud:

https://soundcloud.com/stevenkane-1/sets/woe-is-me

YouTube (playlist):

https://www.youtube.com/playlist?list=PLvwpjZgRH-TC7ETExumulcGjKQ0a_2m8h

YouTube (individual videos):

TV on the Radio: *Trouble*
https://youtu.be/bunJBFtlt-I

EBTG: *The Heart Remains A Child*
https://youtu.be/JIJQF1P_yIs

Judy Garland: *Over The Rainbow*
https://youtu.be/PSZxmZmBfnU

ELO: *Alone In The Universe*
https://youtu.be/VnOkIcvfGfs

Sinead O'Connor: *Sacrifice* **(Elton John cover)**
https://youtu.be/_JEWZRxx9yw

Cat Stevens: *Trouble*
https://youtu.be/NaJPuJ3_hoo

Above & Beyond Present Oceanlab: *Breaking Ties*
https://youtu.be/8cqvuFx9TtI

Beck: *Volcano*
https://youtu.be/6IPt6WVQOjk

Little Feat: *Trouble*
https://youtu.be/kAmQ_FvZISs

Broken Bells: *Citizen*
https://youtu.be/yqnWltpVzsQ

Carly Simon: *It Was So Easy*
https://youtu.be/QpSeK7RkkGU

Beth Orton: *Stars All Seem To Weep*
https://youtu.be/eMM9qhabMds

k.d. lang: *Save Me*
https://youtu.be/JhS_ADeMBIU

The National: *Sorrow*
https://youtu.be/fxWh5ivlBSo

Free at last, Free at last, Thank God almighty, I'm free at last

16 songs, 1 hour 9 minutes

Spotify:

https://open.spotify.com/user/12138164235/playlist/051krc4re8sLjtkmzhSPf7

Soundcloud:

https://soundcloud.com/stevenkane-1/sets/free-at-last-free-at-last

YouTube (playlist):

https://www.youtube.com/playlist?list=PLvwpjZgRH-TA2JPzHZM1p2O7l_FCv7h8t

YouTube (individual videos):

George Harrison: *Ding Dong Ding Dong*
https://youtu.be/SrXswIbWA7Y

Michael Jackson: *Don't Stop Til You Get Enough*
https://youtu.be/yURRmWtbTbo

Novika: *Miss Mood (Satin Jackets Remix)*
https://youtu.be/YYoSj3w6iBc

Jay Z: *On To The Next One*
https://youtu.be/gGYyl-2EuN4

Joe Jackson: *Another World*
https://youtu.be/SYaEpxmhCYU

Sheryl Crow: *My Favorite Mistake*
https://youtu.be/AmIlUKo4dQc

REO Speedwagon: Roll With The Changes
https://youtu.be/jeHkaSHoXw8

Lucinda Williams: *Buttercup*
https://youtu.be/SPsJydmCvS8

Pharrell Williams: *Happy*
https://youtu.be/C7dPqrmDWxs

Soup Dragons: *I'm Free*
https://youtu.be/vqUFwxEc9Dc

Cake: *I Will Survive* **(Gloria Gaynor cover)**
https://youtu.be/f9rCUQjmkxU

Judy Garland: *Get Happy*
https://youtu.be/q7d0NRewzW4

Traveling Wilburys: *End of the Line*
https://youtu.be/UMVjToYOjbM

Gorillaz: *Feel Good Inc.*
https://youtu.be/HyHNuVaZJ-k

Iggy Pop: *Lust for Life*
https://youtu.be/jQvUBf5l7Vw

Frank Sinatra: *That's Life*
https://youtu.be/wonLspauDSc

In-flight entertainment for your breakup

If you want to spend whatever free time you have *still* thinking about relationships, here are some movies, shows, videos and podcasts of interest. There's no consistent point of view or theme—some are comic, some serious, some traditional, some unconventional. Some are awesome, some stink. You decide...

To just click and enjoy these selections—and to make suggestions of other stuff we should add—visit us at GetHappy.Life

Movies

Alice Doesn't Live Here Anymore (1974)

This heart-rendering 1974 movie from writer Robert Getchell, director Martin Scorsese and star Ellen Burstyn (who won the Oscar for Best Actress) is perhaps most well known as the progenitor of the long lived TV sitcom, *Alice*. But if that's all you know about this groundbreaking film, you're in for a huge treat. The story follows the wandering, hopeful, hardscrabble life of single mom, Burstyn, following the accidental death of her husband. But it's not a movie about being a widow or grieving. It's about starting over, going it alone, getting knocked down, and standing up again. It's about the euphoria and awfulness of chasing dreams and pursuing happiness whatever the hell that is from one moment to the next. It's a complicated, modern American tale of the challenges of leaving behind a seemingly preordained, traditional destiny and identity as a "couple," "wife" and "family," and of tackling life, one unpredictable day at a time, as a solo woman in an often misogynist, always shit world. Look for a very young Jodie Foster in (yet another) beautiful, memorable performance, as a misanthropic but honest friend-in-need to Burstyn's confused, angry son.

https://youtu.be/2jFhv9mPqk4

The Best Years of Our Lives (1946)

I'm a film school brat. I *love* movies. When people ask me what are the best movies ever made, this black-and-white oldie always makes my top five. Winner of seven Academy Awards, including Best Picture, Best Director (William Wyler,) Best Screenplay (Robert E. Sherwood), Best Actor (Fredric March), and Best Supporting Actor (Harold Russell,) this is classic, *classic* Hollywood storytelling at its finest. A sprawling, ambitious, multi-layered ensemble piece telling of the difficult readjustments of three soldiers coming home from World War II to their quiet Midwestern town, it's so good, in so many places and ways, I can't really sum it up in such a short review. Caveat: It's from 1946, so there are places where it ages less than perfectly, an at-times somewhat dated, too-neat early 20th century Hollywood view about society, family values, male and female roles, etc. But at the same time, it's eternal. The whole gamut is here: fidelity and infidelity, sex, divorce, physical compatibility, youth and aging, romance, dating, substance abuse, wealth and poverty, growing up and never growing up, parenting, religious faith real and feigned, eternal hope and soul crushing failure, war and peace, economic fairness and inequality. A special, Honorary Academy Award was created just for first-time actor Harold Russell, and believe me, you'll see why. If you don't weep watching this one, you don't have tear ducts. Hell, I get choked up just hearing the first bars of Hugo Friedhofer's Oscar-winning score.

https://youtu.be/1yc5PugV4mk

Bob & Carol & Ted & Alice (1969)

Nominated for several Oscars, this controversial-in-its-time comedy-drama follows the very 1960s, very California relationships of two young married couples, all friends, as they wrestle with changing mores in changing times: affairs, openness, mate swapping and more. A total period piece that sometimes feels, well, a bit foolish—peak swinging 1960's California!—it's surprisingly still resonant, meaningful and funny today, owing to the sincere commitment and warmth of a talented filmmaker (Paul Mazursky) and his all-star cast (Natalie Wood, Robert Culp, Elliott Gould, and Dyan Cannon). One of Mazursky's gifts is somehow bringing out the honest, messy, interesting humanity in scenarios otherwise ripe for silliness or sentimentality, and this movie is a good example of him turning what could have been a ridiculously thin setup into a kind, soulful grown-up drama.

http://fw.to/u7cL75T

Boyhood (2014)

Filmed over 12 years with the same cast by director/writer Richard Linklater, in this unique drama we get to see a boy, Mason, literally grow up, as the same actor, the wonderful Ellar Coltrane, plays him from age seven to eighteen. Mason is a child of split parents, and we get to see family, marriage and divorce as he sees them, over changing times and many evolutions, a moving, sometimes tearful, sometimes funny, sometimes realistically-blase portrait of a contemporary American family— which isn't some kind of aspirationally unchanging group, it's a living organism, easily bruised, with ever developing characters and dynamics. Because the narrative so dramatically, so often leaps ahead in time, some characters and situations feel a little abbreviated, even a little cliched, as there's simply not enough time for deeper characterizations or nuances. But that's a nitpick. There are no stick figures, and no easy good guys and bad guys here. There are real humans, living real, tumultuous, gut wrenching, heart exploding lives. Can you tell I really love this movie? Just the whole idea of keeping a cast together for 12 years just blows my mind in its ambition! What a gem.

https://youtu.be/YooXoxiwOv8

The Break-Up (2006)

Vince Vaughn and Jennifer Aniston play a seriously committed, grown-up couple who live in a condo they own together, at least until the seeming mismatches in their personalities cause them to call it quits. Will they stay broken up? Or does love conquer all? (The couple is not married, but that just seems like a plot contrivance, as the filmmakers didn't want to deal with the subject of marriage and divorce, just compatibility.) This movie makes this list much more for its ambitions and occasional insights than for its overall quality, which suffers from an identity crises: Comedy? Drama? Silly juvenile? Deep and serious? The movie can't make up its mind. And the script and basic conceit aren't that nuanced and the result is tiring. Modern compatibility conflict is a great subject for a movie, and the pairing of Aniston and Vaughn initially feels inspired. But quickly the script feels too cute and shallow, and the performances suffer as a result. And while Aniston and Vaughn are talented comedians, that doesn't serve them well here. Their attempts at emoting can feel like sitcom setups waiting for punchlines. Still, there's a few really good moments too, good-hearted, trenchant illustrations of the perils of saying things like, "you, forever."

https://youtu.be/guRKt55XOfU

Divorce American Style (1967)

Written and produced by Norman Lear a few years before he created *All in the Family*, this 1960s-era attempt at biting satire ages poorly. Given the seemingly blue-ribbon liberal, humanist credentials of its author, as well as that of Lear's partner, the film's director Bud Yorkin, it's odd to watch this movie and realize how misogynistic and hamfisted it is, at least by today's standards. The subject of happiness in long-term relationships and the challenges of divorce are reduced to one, sneering notion: the ostensible unfairness and burden of alimony on men, and the lengths they'll go to be free of such obligations. Perhaps in its original release era, the schemes of the male protagonists came off as clever, and as smart satire (many critics of the time thought highly of the picture and it was nominated for the Best Screenplay Oscar), but today it's just distasteful and unfunny. At best, it's a museum piece, a testament to both how mores and values change over time, and how even the best intentioned people (like the film's creators) can look silly or even malicious when viewed through the lens of far future generations.

https://youtu.be/VYvZpikpljg

Eat Pray Love (2010)

Based on Elizabeth Gilbert's best selling, beloved memoir of the same name, this movie did well in theaters but was trashed by critics who complained that a sincere, thoughtful book had been turned into a self-involved Julia Roberts star-vehicle. I'll just say this: The book is fabulous, a genuine, heartfelt soul-search wrapped in a breathtaking travelogue. It's every wannabee divorcee's fantasy of what life will be like after divorce: Travel the world. Sleep with hot partners. Seek spiritual enlightenment and nirvana at authentic sources. Eat all the pasta you want and still don't mind stepping on a scale. And then fall in love again. Which means Julia Roberts is perfectly cast—she's the somehow simultaneously down-home but super-glam movie star, someone pretty much every wannabee wants to be. And while I agree with critics like Maureen Dowd, who called the movie "navel gazing drivel," I also say, so what. Enjoy. What's wrong with a little self-indulgence, especially if we're feeling blue, and maybe even hopeless, and very, very, very un-indulged. If you can only do one, read the book. If, on the other hand, you only have a couple hours, enjoy the movie, knowing it's a candy-colored Hollywood trifle, that still may poke and prod sensitive spots anyway.

https://youtu.be/mjay5vgIwt4

The Gay Divorcee (1934)

This one's on the list just for the total fun of it. The delightful, classic Hollywood musical features the dazzling Fred Astaire and Ginger Rogers, plus one of my early Hollywood heroes, the hilarious Edward Everett Horton, plus music including Best Original Song Oscar winner *The Continental*, and the timeless masterpiece *Night and Day* by Cole Porter. It's superficially a story of moving on from marriage and divorce. But like most Hollywood musicals, the plot is just a thread on which to hang glamorous people, gorgeous sets and costumes, and breathtaking dance numbers and tunes. Rogers goes to England to engineer an "at fault" setup so she can finally get a divorce from her long lost absent husband. Complications ensue. A fun historical trivia note: The Hays Office, which in the early 20th century oversaw and censored Hollywood movies for controversial ideas, objected to the movie's original title, which came from its source, the Broadway show, *Gay Divorce*. The Hays Office apparently believed it was ok for a person to be gay (happy and light hearted) after getting a divorce, but that the institution of divorce itself should not be considered cheerful. So the producers had to change the name to *The Gay Divorcee*.

https://youtu.be/GV8eUi-fxsc

Enough Said (2013)

The last role played by James Gandolfini before he died, in this film he shines just as brightly as he did as Tony Soprano while completely stepping outside that role. Here he plays a soft spoken, sweet, tentative newly divorced bachelor. Written and directed by the ridiculously talented but under-appreciated Nicole Holofcener, the story follows the travails of Eva, played cheerfully and sensitively by the fabulous Julia Louis-Dreyfus, who is struggling to find love and happiness as a divorced, self-employed masseuse and mom to a teenage daughter. Gandolfini is her on again off again paramour, Albert, a divorcee with a teenage daughter and new-life challenges of his own. There's a clever plot device where Dreyfuss discovers that Gandolfini's ex-wife, played by the always brilliant, frequent Holofcener collaborator Catherine Keener, is her client and good friend—and who loathes her ex-husband Gandolfini. That setup keeps the film amusingly moving along, but the ultimate product is much more than that clever twist. Co-parenting and co-existing with our exes is a major theme, sharply but lovingly handled. Ditto, love and romance post-divorce, and the inevitability and risks of thinking that, at a certain age, we've seen it all. Somehow the independent Holofcener continues to get her smart, poignant productions made and distributed. Thank heavens.

https://youtu.be/nEEJaIjF_Lo

The Kids Are Alright (2010)

Directed and co-written by celebrated indie filmmaker Lisa Cholodenko, this colorful ensemble piece uses a couple of quirky plot twists to blow up a few cherished notions about what makes a family, and what keeps one functional. Released in 2010, it was nominated for Best Picture and Best Screenplay and its stars Annette Bening and Mark Ruffalo for Best Actress and Best Supporting Actor, respectively. (Julianne Moore also stars, and is superb.) The first twist is, the story centers on a normal, conventional family of two parents with two teenage kids... except the parents are lesbians and each kid was born to one of them, but both kids were created using the same sperm donor. Follow? Then the second twist is, the two kids decide they want to know who their father/sperm donor was, and track him down, and lo and behold he lives nearby, and, played by Ruffalo, he's a super cool, nice guy. And he's actually happy when they find them. But is he their parent? The two moms are not thrilled to even have to think about that. But Ruffalo gets sucked in and meddles, causing tension. But maybe that's ok: He's just so sensitive, self-effacing and charming. But then he has a sexual affair with Moore. Then things get really heated. For Moore's not only a cheater, it appears she's bi-sexual. It's complicated. But super well done. This is a unique, special movie. See it.

https://youtu.be/RixlpHKfb6M

Kramer vs. Kramer (1979)

I watched this again recently and was I glad I did. Nominated for nine Academy Awards, winner of five including Best Picture, Best Director (Sidney Lumet,) Best Actor (Dustin Hoffman), Best Screenplay (Robert Benton,) and Best Supporting Actress (Meryl Streep,) this 1979 drama was amongst the first major Hollywood products to try to realistically, and non-judgmentally, address modern marriage and divorce—and though controversial at the time amongst feminists, also the subjects of misogyny and the struggles of females to live in a male dominated world. The story tells of the blow up of the marriage of Hoffman and Streep, as Streep seemingly abruptly abandons ship, leaving behind her crushed young son with her overwhelmed ex-husband. The utter magnificence of this movie is not just in all the usual places—the wonderful script, fantastic but unobtrusive direction, spectacular performances—but also in the amazing way the film does not devolve into some obvious, pedantic TV-movie-of-the-week, as its plot and even title seem to suggest. Streep won her (first) Oscar for playing a mother who tears herself apart when she abandons her young child. That seemingly unconventional-for-the-sake-of-being-unconventional conceit could easily have devolved into a Cruella DeVille caricature. But no, all the Oscars are richly deserved, not least for making Streep's character entirely human and heart-crushingly sympathetic. (Streep famously rewrote many parts of the script herself.) Likewise Hoffman's character, who goes from anger and self-involvement to vulnerability and deeply felt loving commitment. Marriage, divorce, parenting, personal freedoms, the pursuit of happiness, aging, settling for less or not settling for less, all these topics and more are sensitively, artfully explored.

https://youtu.be/3SP9n13ux1I

Network (1976)

One of the most successful and celebrated movies in the history of Hollywood, and the perhaps crowning achievement of Paddy Chayefsky, one of the most revered motion picture authors ever, *Network* is a dark satire of modern tech and media businesses and their profound effects on humanity. The winner of four Oscars, it's not really a film about marriage and relationships per se, but, then again, it is. Chayefsky's breathtaking, piercing talents as a writer can accomplish in one scene what other artists labor to communicate in entire careers. While I highly, highly recommend watching the entire film, in particular check out the scene (spoiler alert, sort of) where William Holden tells his wife of 25 years, Beatrice Straight, he's leaving her for another woman. Straight won an Oscar for Best Supporting Actress basically just for this scene (she's not in the movie much otherwise) and it's so well deserved. Somehow Chayefsky, brilliant director Sidney Lumet, Holden and Straight pack what feels like an entire story of a deep, long and complex marriage into one thrilling, excruciating scene. It's a stunning centerpiece to a stunning film, an emotional volcano that instantly centers and humanizes an otherwise cool, cerebral movie. A caveat: Today, 40+ years later, some may criticize Chayefsky for a somewhat dated, male-centric view of midlife and marriage crises. What do you think?

https://youtu.be/rhgsfn7CtDw

https://youtu.be/1cSGvqQHpjs

The Parent Trap (1961; remake 1998)

A silly, cheerful, antique trifle that, in my opinion, in today's world borders on being deeply offensive, this very-old-school 1961 Disney "family" movie should be banned from families, and homes experiencing divorce. Or, at least, if that's you, probably best not to have your kids watch it. Or, if they do, figure out how to explain that it has about as much to do with reality as Peter Pan. Or as Stalinist propaganda. That aside, if you can turn off the thinking part of your brain and just focus on the popcorn and candy in your lap, the original version starring Hayley Mills, Brian Keith and Maureen O'Hara is a kind of distilled classic of the sort of ostensibly family-friendly, technicolor nonsense peddled with a patronizing smile by corporate America on young baby boomers, I guess to curdle their brains and keep them happily consuming. No wonder they all turned on, tuned in and dropped out. The 1998 remake blows my mind in so many ways: How truly awful a movie can be. How stupid producers, studios and even brilliant artists like writer-director Nancy Meyers can be in their choice of films to remake. How the managers and agents who supposedly were looking out for the amazingly talented, innocent child Lindsay Lohan were actually a bunch of sinister predators who should be flogged in public.

https://youtu.be/pyqzkhBJds4

https://youtu.be/2KKHuqUWW3Y

Stepmom (1998)

Stock up big-time on tissues and hankies for this one. Terminally ill divorcee Susan Sarandon has to somehow acclimate her kids and herself to the fact that the children are getting a new stepmother, their father and Sarandon's former husband Ed Harris's younger, inexperienced new partner, Julia Roberts. And the two kids just don't love Dad's new lover. And Sarandon is faltering, her mortal time rapidly running out. Granted, this is a very, by-the-book, manipulative, corny Hollywood tearjerker. Having Sarandon be terminally ill makes what would have been a really poignant, difficult, modern family tale—a divorced parent dealing with the fact that her kids now have more than two "parents"—into an at times maudlin, sudsy soap opera. But whatever: It's just a really good Hollywood sob story movie that doesn't pretend to be anything else. And its leads are all first rate performers, movie stars at the tops of their games. So despite it being a well-oiled weep-sucking machine, in it's smaller, quieter moments, the film manages some worthwhile observations on modern relationships and parenting. And of course, a really, really good cry.

https://youtu.be/Z73WMzLjtvU

War of the Roses (1989)

Unfortunately, this is a short review so I'm limited in how many bad things I can say about this turd. Michael Douglas and Kathleen Turner are going through such a nasty divorce, they fight—literally, bite, claw and scratch each other and destroy everything and everyone—brawling over who gets their beautiful house. Maybe the Farrelly brothers could have turned this into some kind of looney slapstick fun, but director Danny DeVito and his august cast take themselves way too seriously, as if

253

they're making some dark, biting satire. They're not. The script and the drama are thin, a fortune cookie masquerading as deep thoughts. Yes, some critics really liked this movie, but then again, some critics like individually wrapped cheese food slices. Maybe there was an embryo of a sensitive, decent idea at the outset—the film is based on a novel (that I haven't read)—but the final result is just a self-aggrandizing mishmash spectacle, of Hollywood elite preening like they're savvy social observers, while getting paid a ton just to gleefully smash expensive scenery. Some movies are so bad they're good. This one? Just bad.

https://youtu.be/Z3gYqHVMndE

The Way Way Back (2013)

This movie stars Liam James, Steve Carell, Toni Collette, Allison Janney, AnnaSophia Robb, Sam Rockwell, Maya Rudolph, Rob Corddry and Amanda Peet. Do I even need to say more? The quirky, charming, sometimes melancholy story follows a 14 year old boy, Duncan, through his unlikely summer at Cape Cod with his distracted, partying mom, Pam, her dubious, wealthy boyfriend, Trent, and Trent's condescending daughter, Steph. A motley quasi-family unit, if ever there was one. Largely ignored by everyone, Duncan stumbles into the small-time local water amusement park, Water Wizz, and there finds his home of sorts, as he's befriended and mentored by the oddball characters who work in the park. For those not old enough to get the reference, the movie's title refers to the far rear section of a station wagon, behind the back seats, where younger kids often rode, back in the good old days before anyone cared about things like safety belts. And that's fitting, as this tender film shows us a child's bumpy ride, and through his eyes, a strange, scary but still wonderful world, as Duncan settles into a different family life than he ever envisioned, while discovering an inner strength and wisdom he never imagined, either.

https://youtu.be/6qoaVUdbWMs

Teachers, Thinkers, Advice

ChopperPapa

Subtitled, "A Husband, Man and Dad Blog," ChopperPapa is the at times edgy-funny, at times gut-wrenching and tough-love musings of Kyle Bradford, containing what he calls "observations and discussions about marriage, single parenting, dating, divorce, and manhood." Bradford talks candidly and often about his own history and life experiences—his own difficult divorce and struggles to co-parent his two young children—but the material isn't memoir. It's a series of pointed reflections on the modern male experience of love and parenthood, and reinvention, stumbling and recovering—and stumbling again. And motorcycles. (That's the "chopper" part.) Bradford has a distinctive voice. He's sensitive and gentle but also a little gruff, very, well, male. And that's his intention, and strength. He's progressive and modern, and unafraid to challenge conventional wisdom, while at the same time he's unabashedly of the view that gender can really matter, and men and women can be equal while also being different. In the same vein, Bradford also produces and hosts the podcast "Fatherhood Wide Open," where he interviews male authors and thinkers.

http://chopperpapa.com/2017/06/divorce-selfies-insignificance-marriage/#more-9173

http://bewideopen.com/

Esther Perel (1999-ongoing)

Esther Perel is the Belgian-born psychotherapist and bestselling author of *Mating in Captivity: Unlocking Erotic Intelligence* (2006) and *The State of Affairs: Rethinking Infidelity (2017)*. In my opinion, she is the single most original, inspiring, brilliant and influential investigator today of modern emotional and romantic relationships. A still-practicing couples therapist based in New York City, she combines scientific diligence with a huge heart; she is sensitive, non-judgemental and caring while also sharp and pointed in her at-times extremely unconventional views. Maybe start with her wildly popular, brief TED Talk videos. I find her podcast series, *Where Should We Begin*, much less satisfying. The podcasts are all more-or-less unedited recordings of actual couples-therapy sessions. The names of the participants are not shared but everything else is. The premise is fascinating, but the listening much less so. In therapy, we all ramble on. And on. A good therapist doesn't cut anyone short, and Perel is a good therapist. The result is too much of a good thing. I abandoned ship after two episodes, longing for Perel to substantially edit the recordings and interject her own commentary. But that's a quibble. Perel is a genius, I think, and her brave, groundbreaking work is a treasure.

https://www.estherperel.com/

https://youtu.be/sa0RUmGTCYY

https://youtu.be/P2AUat93a8Q

https://youtu.be/s7E9ASb3LfE

Reboot.io

Reboot is a coaching company with a focus on improving one's relationship with work to lead to growth as individuals. But anyone can get huge delight and benefits from their offerings, and from their stimulating, sometimes gut-wrenching thesis that we use "radical self inquiry"—deliberate, methodical examination and deconstruction of the self—to achieve personal growth. Combining practical advice with a heady, cheerful mix of modern and ancient philosophy, poetry, and non-judgemental love, stirred with a dollop of the Buddhist quest for enlightenment, Reboot's founders and network offer all sorts of counsel and wisdom, even if you never enroll in their programs. Check out their web site and try one of their podcasts. The material's largely geared towards workplace issues and that may be enough for you, but look for the other gems, too. One of my favorite podcasts is titled, "Building Relational Trust." (Sound useful here?) In that 50 minute conversation, Reboot founder Jerry Colonna interviews one of his own coaches and mentors, author, educator, and activist Parker Palmer, whose intense wisdom, clear perception and deep love of humanity comes wrapped in an endearingly gentle, understated, wry, Midwestern sensibility. Colonna and Palmer talk a lot about "leaders" but substitute "parents" or "spouses" and the ideas are just as resonant. Full disclosure: I'm a longtime friend of Colonna, have worked with him as a coach, and have been a participant in Reboot events.

https://www.reboot.io/episode/42-building-relational-trust-parker-palmer/

Savage Lovecast (1991-ongoing)

Dan Savage is a treasure. Idiosyncratic but mainstream, tender and sensitive but grouchy and tough, caustically active on behalf of LGBTQ causes but a source of love and smarts to the entire universe, gay straight or otherwise, Savage created and writes *Savage Love,* an internationally syndicated relationship and sex advice column, and also writes and hosts the popular podcast of the same name. He's an original, and also an original gangsta: he's been a leading light in the love and relationship advice game since 1991. It's hard to imagine a topic he hasn't covered. Twice. But he nevertheless manages to keep it fresh and interesting and punchy and funny and sometimes, a little raw.

https://www.savagelovecast.com/

https://www.thestranger.com/authors/259/dan-savage

Dear Sugars

Originally an advice column with a cult following in the independent magazine *The Rumpus*, now co-produced by NPR and *The New York Times*, *Dear Sugars* is a podcast that bills itself as a "radically empathic advice show." I genuinely like this series but I'm not sure I can vouch for that description. Well-known authors Cheryl Strayed and Steve Almond host the podcast, and they are polished pros, but, personally, at times I find them not entirely empathic, and occasionally a bit judgemental, too quick to decide the underlying truth of a situation or who's right and who's wrong. But, in their defense, maybe it's because their show format is that they respond to listeners' emails, so they only get a quick glimpse and summary of the people and dilemmas they mull over. And, of course, just one side of a conflict. Or maybe it's because they've seen and heard so gosh darned much—separately or together they've been offering relationship advice for many, many years. Still, they're always sensitive, caring and open-minded, and never fall into predictable male/female roles, and are bracingly candid about their own checkered personal histories. Best, they often have really superb guests on with them. One great example: novelist Susan Cheever, who steals the show and turns the hosts upside down and inside out in the 2016 episode "The Infidelity Episodes Part 4: The Other Woman." It's so interesting and unexpected, I listened to it twice.

https://www.nytimes.com/podcasts/dear-sugars

http://www.wbur.org/dearsugar/2017/05/26/dear-sugar-episode-fifty-two-rerun

DivorceForce

Founded by two men in the confusing throes of their own divorces, DivorceForce is a relatively new venture that offers a web- and mobile app-based social network for people who are divorcing, divorced, or being impacted by divorce, or other changing families and relationships. In the company's words, the network is focused on offering "Education," "Connection," and "Support." That is, users can gain knowledge, meet others in similar circumstances, and have a shoulder to lean on when times are tough. Caveat, I have not spent a huge amount of hours on DivorceForce—I'm now years past my divorce and don't really need this right now—but I have spent some time perusing their offerings, and, as of this writing, I give the platform an A+ for vision and ambition, and a B+ for execution. And that less-than-perfect score is largely from the "chicken and egg problem": It's hard to have a successful social network without a lot of participants, but it's hard to get folks to use a social network that isn't yet full of other people. But no matter. Even if not yet full to the brim, there is still lots of useful stuff and people right now in the DivorceForce network. The free version offers limited access to some material and features, and with a paid subscription you get a much more elaborate, full blown networking platform and resource.

TV

All in the Family (1971-1979)

As the name suggests, this celebrated, groundbreaking TV sitcom is specifically about relationships. Various modern marriages are at its core: The cantankerous, middle-aged, blue-collar bigot Archie Bunker and his traditional, mousey, subservient wife Edith. The Bunkers' 1970s-liberated daughter Gloria and her progressive son-of-immigrants husband Michael Stivic. The upwardly mobile but justifiably paranoid African-American couple next door, gruff George and loving but rough and ready Louise Jefferson. Still, despite the series well-earned reputation for smartly, sensitively taking on all sorts of complicated and challenging subjects, viewed today it's attitude towards marriage is still pretty standard, saccharine fare, I think. Everything gets resolved neatly by every episode's end and the couples kiss and makeup and snuggle. There's one episode specifically about divorce, "Amelia's Divorce," from the 1975 season, which, for me anyways, simultaneously nails it and falls short at the same time, as it's all just an excuse for Archie and Edith to realize how much they really do love each other (and kiss, makeup and snuggle). Well, such was the tenor of those times—unlike today, 40 years ago no TV network or producer would have a married couple at the center of a huge smash hit TV show realize anything else. In any case, that particular episode is still resonant, as it reveals how Edith's visiting cousins have a seemingly fabulous marriage that's really a toxic cauldron of resentment. Over so many episodes, this series brilliantly, delicately, often hilariously, explores a wide variety of realistic relationships and people.

https://youtu.be/tWzEj1o4PBk

An American Family (1973)

Arguably the first ever "reality TV" show, this landmark documentary series shocked and titillated pretty much the entire

USA when it originally aired in 1973 (on PBS, no less). The premise was simple: a film crew moved in and lived with a family, unobtrusively and neutrally observing the everyday lives of the Louds of Santa Barbara, CA, who were selected, it was said, as a reasonable approximation of a typical (white, upper middle class) American household of the time. Unlike "reality" shows of today, *An American Family* was entirely unscripted, but after it aired there were bitter disputes between the Louds and the producers over whether the material had been unfairly edited, or situations somehow architected, manipulated to create and inflame tensions and, ergo, heighten drama and increase ratings. (Ya think?) In any case, these allegedly pedestrian lives were anything but. Son Lance Loud comes out to his parents, revealing he's gay, a milestone and first for American TV and popular culture. Arguably even more startling, in a testy, memorable exchange, after 21 years of marriage Pat Loud asks her husband Bill for a divorce and to leave the house. With all the noise coming off all the screens we live with today, it's hard to imagine how powerfully a single show, aired once, could simultaneously unite and divide an entire nation. But, for a few months in early 1973, this one did.

https://youtu.be/MJ-yofcaPMk

Divorce (2016 - continuing)

I was so excited when I heard this HBO series was coming. I'm a big Sarah Jessica Parker fan and avidly watched the *Sex in the City* series, every episode, as it first aired. And I also adore Parker's costar here, Thomas Haden Church. And I thought, well, it's about time for some smart, funny, sensitive artists to take on the subject of divorce, and in an ongoing series format, where all sorts of characters and issues can be given time to breathe and develop deeply. And it was to be a comedy, so much the better: Nobody wants to see some syrupy, too-serious mopey drama about divorce, but a comic approach could tackle all sorts of touchy stuff. So it's that much more disappointing to have to report: for me, this series is a dud. Stick figure characters, silly cliched situations, cheap attempts for laughs that fall flat, ugh. Double ugh. I even watched several episodes thinking it can't possibly stay that bad, but it did. Paging Darren Star and Candace Bushnell... Paging Darren Star and Candace Bushnell...

https://youtu.be/CGxlK6yQugY

Happily Divorced (2011-2013)

In general, I'm a big fan of Fran Drescher, who I find refreshingly authentic, self-effacing, and funny. But I have mixed feelings about this series, which seems to try way too hard to be funny and never lets the interesting setup just develop and blossom. Based loosely on her own life, the premise is, series star and creator Drescher's eighteen year marriage breaks up when her husband comes out as gay. But they're financially strapped, so they keep living together and are forced to reinvent their relationship and discover who each of them really is. For me, this should not have been a traditional, live-audience, multi-camera studio sitcom. It should have been shot on film, one camera, no live audience, no need for constant laugh lines. Just let the interesting flesh and blood characters get on with their lives and go to humor, pathos or tears as situations require. Instead, in tiresome sitcom fashion, it's often big joke after big joke, some oddly crude and tone deaf, and all underlined by an annoying, guffawing laugh track. Still, as I said, I have a big place in my heart for Drescher and when occasionally she shines, she's fabulously bright.

https://youtu.be/zhAcvkomv98

Modern Family (2009 - continuing)

Well, how can I make a list like this and not include the aptly named *Modern Family*? And I'll just plain say it: I frigging love this show. It's screamingly original and well done, plus laugh out loud funny while also occasionally being meaningful, insightful and poignant on the subject we're all here to mull over: what constitutes love and family and a healthy relationship in these frantic, confusing, modern times. I will nitpick, however: I find this series portrayal of divorce to be less satisfying than its portrayal of most everything else. The writers fall back on easy TV sitcom cliches, e.g. how the divorced main characters' exes are all so batshit crazy (e.g., Ed O'Neill's ex wife, played by Shelley Long) or cold and unlovable (Sofia Vergara's ex husband, played by Benjamin Bratt) that, of course, we don't care about them at all, which makes it so easy for us to root for the main characters in their second marriage, and not have any painful questions about, say, why their first marriages tanked, or why these arguably super important people are almost never in the story, always offscreen, rarely in their children's lives. In a similar cliche sitcom fashion, relationships have travails but nothing too serious—everyone kisses and makes up by every episode's end. But who cares! This series is fabulous, brilliant, and bursting with good cheer and hysterical humor. Love it, love it, love it.

https://youtu.be/oITvfgeQNbA

A Breakup & Divorce Cookbook

If we're in an unhappy relationship or breakup, we need our strength. Physical stamina, but psychic and emotional fortitude, too. Food is good medicine for all. And when I say medicine I don't necessarily mean "healthy." When I'm low, a dose of chocolate heals me much better than kale.

In any case, here my Advisors, friends and I offer a few recipes for blue moods. We tag them as follows:

(H) **Healthy**   When your body needs to be nursed.
(C) **Comfort**   Food for fun.
(E) **Entertaining**   You're in a funk but peeps food.

For more recipes and to add your own please visit us online at GetHappy.Life

Aunt Felice's Banana Bread (C) (E)

Ingredients:

- 3-4 overripe bananas
- ¼ c. melted butter
- 1 c. sugar
- 1 ½ c. flour
- 1 egg
- 1 tsp. Baking soda
- 1 tsp salt
- Optional: Chocolate chips to taste (but is chocolate ever really optional?)

Instructions:

1. Preheat oven to 325 degrees.
2. Mash bananas with a fork in a bowl.
3. Stir in remaining ingredients.
4. Pour into buttered glass loaf pan, 8 ½ x 4 ½ x 2 ½-inch.
5. Bake 55-60 minutes.

Note: Anytime bananas get overripe, freeze them then defrost them in the microwave for this recipe. The thawed bananas have a lot of liquid that makes the banana bread very moist. It's a great way to now throw out good bananas and always have them available to make banana bread!

—*Lisa Hodes*

Avocado Toast with Pomegranate Seeds (H) (C) (E)

Serves 8.

Ingredients:

- 8 slices bread, lightly toasted
- 4 ripe avocados, peeled and pits removed
- juice of 2 limes
- 1 cucumber, peeled and finely chopped
- salt and pepper to taste
- 1 cup pomegranate seeds
- 1 cup fresh tarragon or your favorite fresh herb

Instructions:

1. Dice avocados and mash with lime juice, salt and pepper.
2. Fold in chopped cucumber.
3. Spread seasoned avocado on to toast and top generously with pomegranate seeds and fresh tarragon

—Andy Goldfarb

Baked Salami (C) (E)

Ingredients:

- 1 large kosher salami
- 1 large jar duck sauce

Instructions:

1. Place salami (whole) in casserole dish and pour duck sauce all over.
2. Bake at 375 degrees for 2-3 hours.
3. Baste occasionally with duck sauce.
4. Serve with mustard.

—Lisa Hodes

Breakfast Casserole (C) (E)

Ingredients:

- Tater tots
- 2 cups whole milk
- 1 lb tube of Jimmy Dean Regular Sausage
- 4 tbsp flour
- 1+ cup cheddar cheese
- 3 scallions

Instructions:

1. Preheat oven to 375. Butter a 8X11 baking dish. Cover bottom with tater tots. Place in oven to start cooking.
2. Brown sausage and break up over medium heat. Once it's cooked through, sprinkle flour over top. Cover with milk and stir until thick.
3. Remove tater tots from oven. Sprinkle with half of the cheese and half of the chopped scallions. Pour sausage mixture over the top. Cover with remainder of cheese and scallions and return to the oven until the whole thing is gooey and bubbly.
4. Savor the yumminess.

—Kiva Schuler

Butternut Squash Lasagna (H) (C) (E)

Serves 10-12

Ingredients:

- 1 box lasagna noodles (1 lb, pre-cooked dried if possible)
- 2 medium-sized butternut squash (roasted, peeled, seeds removed and rough chopped - about 8 cups. or you can buy already prepped at the supermarket)

- 1 cup fresh sage
- 2 tbsp honey
- 1 lb frozen spinach, defrosted and water squeezed out
- 1 cup mascarpone cheese
- 3 cups fresh mozzarella cheese, grated
- 2 cups parmesan cheese, grated (1/2 cup for ricotta mixture, 1-1/2 cups to sprinkle over layers)
- 2 quarts ricotta cheese (two containers)
- 1 egg, lightly beaten
- 2 tsp salt
- pepper to taste

Prepare the lasagna:

4. Preheat oven to 375 degrees.
5. Roast butternut squash whole for 1 hour or until you can easily pierce with a knife.
6. Meanwhile, in a mixing bowl combine the ricotta cheese, 1/2 cup parmesan cheese and egg. Set aside.
7. When squash is cooked, let cool slightly, cut in half horizontally, peel, remove the seeds and roughly chop.
8. Place squash, mascarpone, sage, honey, salt and pepper in a food processor or blender and pulse, leaving some chunks of squash for texture.

Layer the lasagna:

1. In a 3 quart or 4.8 quart lasagna pan, make layers of butternut squash puree, spinach, ricotta mixture, parmesan, mozzarella and lasagna sheets until pan is full (3-4 layers). Do not put mozzarella on the top of lasagna until it has baked for 45 minutes covered with aluminum foil. Then add mozzarella and bake uncovered for an additional 15 minutes or until mozzarella is melted and slightly brown.
2. Let cool for 30 minutes before cutting slices.

Note: You can assemble the lasagna a day ahead and refrigerate, unbaked. Or you can bake, let cool, refrigerate and reheat. Lasagna tastes even better the next day.

—Andy Goldfarb

Chicken Cacciatore (H) (C) (E)

Ingredients:

- 1 chicken, cut into 1/8's
- 4 T. olive oil
- 2 small boxes sliced mushrooms
- 2 envelopes or cubes beef bouillon (mixed with 1/2 cup water)
- Pinch oregano
- 2 T. Gravy Master
- 1 large can tomato paste
- 4 cloves of garlic, mashed
- Salt and pepper to taste

Instructions:

1. In a large skillet over high heat, brown chicken pieces in olive oil.
2. Remove chicken.
3. Saute mushrooms. If there's too much oil in the pan, drain some out.
4. Add bouillon, oregano, gravy master, tomato paste, garlic and salt and pepper. Mix well.
5. Put chicken back in pan, mix well, cover and simmer for 1 to 1 1/4 hours.
6. Serve over rice or noodles.

—Lisa Hodes

Jewish Penicillin (aka, Chicken Soup) (H) (C) (E)

Ingredients:

- 1 whole chicken
- 1-2 lbs of chicken wings or legs
- 1 lb carrots
- ½ lb parsnips
- ½ lb celery
- 2 large onions
- 4 tbsp peppercorns
- 2 bay leaves

Instructions:

1. Place everything except ½ the carrots and the wings or legs into a big pot and cover with water. Salt generously. I also appreciate adding the neck and organs for some extra depth of flavor.
2. Bring to boil then reduce to simmer and cover. Cook for 2 hours. Remove chicken from pot and allow to cool, replacing with legs/wings.
3. Cook for another 1-2 hours. Drain stock into large bowl, discarding all of the remnants.
4. Shred cooked chicken, slice remaining carrots. Add back to broth and serve with your favorite accoutrement... Matzo Balls, Egg Noodles and Wild Rice are some of our favs.

Note: Cures everything.

—*Kiva Schuler*

Cinnamon Carrots (H) (C) (E)

Ingredients:

- One bag of carrots
- Butter
- Cinnamon

Instructions:

1. Cut up a bag of carrots into bite size chunk.
2. Place in sauce pan with a ½ stick of butter and cover with water.
3. Add 1 tbsp of cinnamon.
4. Cook until water evaporates.

Yummy, comfort-y, sweet tooth snacking... and healthy.

—Kiva Schuler

DoorDash (C) (E)

Ingredients:

- One cell phone
- The DoorDash app, or equivalent (there are a few)
- One credit card
- Your finger
- *Optional: plates and silverware*

Instructions:

1. If you don't already have it, download DoorDash app. Launch the app.
2. If you don't have one, use your credit card to create a DoorDash account. Include your home address or wherever you want the grub sent to.

3. Pick a restaurant from the app's big list. Maybe try someplace new. Or maybe just get the same burrito and nachos you get every night. Actually, now that I think about it, I don't really care what you get. You're hungry. You should eat. That's what matters.
4. Peruse the menus. Place take-out order.
5. Wait 15-30 minutes, or until the order arrives. It doesn't matter how often you check the time or stare at the app. It doesn't arrive quicker. On the other hand, who knows.
6. Insert face deep into the take-out order bag. Inhale deeply. Yes! Food!
7. Decide whether to use your real plates and silverware, or what the heck, just scarf it all down using the plastic utensils and the paper bag that came with it.

Note: Goes well with "Ice cream, from the container." See below.

—Steve Kane

Frosted Flakes with milk and banana (C)

Ingredients:

- Frosted Flakes
- Milk (any kind)
- One ripe banana

Instructions:

1. Pour Frosted Flakes into a bowl. Do not fill bowl to the brim—you need room for the banana and milk!
2. Peel banana. Cut away bruised areas and pull off and discard those annoying stringy things, as well as the little stump at the bottom. (Unless you really like those stringy things and the stump, in which case, go ahead and eat them, but I think you're gross.)
3. Slice banana into round slices approximately ¼" thick.
4. Place slices onto Frosted Flakes.

5. Pour in milk. Optional: With your spoon, tap down cereal and banana slices so they get wet with milk.

Note: Some people like to pour on the milk before slicing the banana. This results in a nice, slightly soggier cereal, but requires speedy banana slicing and eating to avoid the mix becoming mush. Unless you like mush.

Second note: I find Frosted Flakes to be the quintessential cereal to eat with milk and banana, but heck, it's a free country so, go ahead, go wild, and experiment, say, with Honey Nut Cheerios. Or Captain Crunch. And go ahead and use whole milk. So smooth and rich. And we know now all that stuff about removing fat from our diets is basically bunk.

Third note: Tastes just as delicious eaten standing up, watching TV. Just don't drip on your shirt. Anyways, not if you're going to sleep in it. Or at least, not if you're going to sleep in it in the same bed as me. Sour milk smells!

—Steve Kane

Grilled PB and Banana Sandwich (C)

Ingredients:
- 2 pieces of bread
- ½ a banana
- Peanut butter
- Regular butter (the more the better)

Instructions:
1. Make a PB&B sandwich.
2. Slather both pieces of bread with butter.
3. Grill on medium heat until warmed through and browned.

—Kiva Schuler

Ice Cream from the Container (C)

Ingredients:

- Any pre-packaged container of ice cream
- A spoon
- Kitchen rag or paper towels

Instructions:

1. Open container of ice cream
2. Use kitchen rag or paper towels to hold ice cream container to keep hand from getting too cold.
3. Use spoon to eat ice cream directly from container. *Optional: For each bite, try to get a good mix of ice cream plus any candy or other chunks in the ice cream.*
4. Use kitchen rag or paper towels to clean your face and any drips on the furniture. Or don't, whatever, just leave it until whenever.
5. Wrap dirty spoon in kitchen rag or paper towels so it doesn't stick to the carpet, couch or coffee table. Unless you already put the spoon down somewhere, then who cares.
6. When you're done, put the lid back on whatever ice cream is left and place container in the freezer. Or just leave it out. Maybe you'll eat the whole thing. Taking a brief pause makes you feel less guilty, sometimes. Or maybe not. But if it melts you can always get more. Or just drink it with some ice tomorrow morning for breakfast.

—*Steve Kane*

Louisa's Kugel (Noodle Pudding) (C) (E)

Ingredients:
- 12-oz bag wide egg noodles
- 1 container cottage cheese (16 oz)
- 1 container sour cream (16 oz)
- 8 oz cream cheese, room temperature
- 4 eggs, lightly beaten
- 3/4 cup sugar
- 1 tsp vanilla
- pinch of salt
- 1 tbsp cinnamon + extra for dusting on top
- 2 cup raisins, golden or dark
- 1 cup slivered almonds
- 1 12-oz jar apricot jam
- 2 tbsp butter + extra for buttering the pan

Instructions:
1. Preheat oven to 350°.
2. Coat 9" x 13" (3-quart) baking dish with butter.
3. Cook noodles according to package directions. Strain and set aside.
4. Break eggs into a large bowl and whisk.
5. Add dairy products to the bowl and mix.
6. Gently fold in cooked noodles.
7. Mix in vanilla, sugar and cinnamon.
8. Fold in raisins.
9. Pour mixture into baking dish.
10. In a separate pan, heat apricot jam for 1 minute until the jam melts then pour jam over noodle mixture and spread with a pastry brush.
11. Sprinkle slivered almonds on top, dust with cinnamon, dot with small pieces of butter, cover with tin foil and bake for 50 minutes.
12. Uncover and bake for an additional 10 minutes so the top is slightly crunchy.
13. Let cool slightly as it will be easier to serve. Serves 12-14

—*Andy Goldfarb*

Monte Cristo Sandwich (C)

This delicious concoction takes minutes to prepare, is perfect for breakfast, lunch or dinner, and vies with the Chicken Parmesan Sub for the title of Greatest Comfort Food Sandwich Of All Time.

Ingredients:

- ButterEggs
- Sliced bread
- Milk
- Sliced ham
- Sliced turkey
- Sliced swiss cheese
- Powdered sugar or maple syrup (optional)

Instructions:

1. Make French Toast
   a. Melt butter in a frying pan over low heat
   b. Break eggs into a large bowl, add a little milk and whisk or beat until consistent.
   c. Soak sliced bread in eggs and milk mixture
   d. Fry soaked bread slices in frying pan until golden brown
2. Place sliced cheese onto golden brown french toast slices and cover frying pan briefly to melt cheese
3. Remove French Toast slices with melted cheese from frying pan and place, open faced, onto a plate
4. Place sliced ham and sliced turkey into frying pan to quickly sear and heat up meats
5. Place meats on open faced French Toast with melted cheese and then close up to form sandwich
6. Season lightly with powdered sugar (optional)
7. Serve with maple syrup (optional)
8. Garnish with a Kosher Dill pickle spear (optional)

—Steve Kane

Pasta Bolognese (C) (E)

Ingredients:

- 1 lb ground lamb
- 1 lb ground beef or veal
- 4 carrots
- 4 stalks celery
- 3 cloves garlic
- 1 red onion
- 1 1/2 cups good red wine
- 2 cans peeled plum tomatoes
- 3 tbsp tomato paste
- ½ cup whole milk
- Pasta of choice

Instructions:

1. Dice the onion and mince the garlic.
2. Brown in oil over medium heat for 10 minutes until onions are wilted.
3. Add wine and allow to almost completely reduce - about 15-20 minutes.
4. Once sauce has reduced add tomatoes, breaking up with your hands, and their juice to pot.
5. Add tomato paste and ⅔ cup of water.
6. Bring to boil and then reduce to simmer.
7. Cook uncovered for 1 hour.
8. In a skillet brown meats, while breaking up.
9. Salt and pepper generously.
10. Add diced carrots and celery.
11. Add to tomato sauce and simmer for one more hour.
12. Add milk and cook 15 more minutes on

Serve over some pasta with grated parmesan.

—*Kiva Schuler*

Pasta with Butter and Fried Chicken (C) (E)

Ingredients:

- Pasta (any kind)
- Fully cooked, take-out fried chicken pieces or nuggets
- Butter
- Salt

Instructions:

9. Put water and a little salt in a pot.
10. Boil water.
11. Cook pasta in boiling water.
12. While pasta is cooking, shred chicken pieces into small morsels. Include skin but discard bones and cartilage.
13. Heat chicken morsels in microwave until warm.
14. When pasta is cooked, drain it in a colander and rinse it with hot water to get rid of stickiness. Rinse the cooking pot with hot water to also clean it of stickiness while keeping the pot hot.
15. Put generous amount of butter in the still warm pot and place it on low heat on the stove until butter melts.
16. Put pasta and chicken in the pot.
17. Stir until everything is mixed well and coated with melted butter.

Just as delicious eaten directly out of the cooking pot. And less cleaning up that way!

—*Steve Kane*

Pasta with Ragu (C)

Ingredients:
- Pasta (any kind)
- Jar of Ragu Traditional (the original)

Instructions:
1. Put water and a little salt in a pot.
2. Boil water.
3. Cook pasta in boiling water.
4. When pasta is cooked, drain it in a colander and rinse it with hot water to get rid of stickiness. Rinse the cooking pot with hot water to also clean it of stickiness while keeping the pot hot.
5. Put the pasta back in the pot.
6. Pour the Ragu sauce over the pasta until every piece is lightly coated and there is a little extra on the bottom of the pot.
7. Stir until everything is mixed well and coated evenly.

Note: My children loved to put "sprinkle cheese" (grated parmesan) on their pasta although I always preferred it without.

Second Note: As an option, saute ground beef and add to the sauce prior to pouring over the pasta for variety and to add protein.

—*Laura W. Campbell*

Swedish Meatballs (H) (C) (E)

Ingredients:

- Hamburger
- Heinz Chili Sauce
- Welch's Grape Jelly
- Heinz Ketchup

Instructions:

1. Mix sauce
2. Add meatballs
3. Cook for one hour
4. Simmer for one hour

—Andy Goldfarb

Tacos (C) (E)

Ingredients:

- Old El Paso Taco Kit
- Ground beef
- Ortega Taco Sauce
- Head of Iceberg Lettuce
- Tomatoes
- Bag of Grated Mexican Four Cheeses

Instructions:

1. Saute ground beef with the taco seasoning packet from the taco kit
2. While meat is sauteing, cut up both the iceberg lettuce and the tomatoes, put each in its own bowl
3. Put the grated cheese in a bowl
4. Place taco shells on a separate plate
5. When meat is cooked thoroughly, place in a large bowl
6. Place all of the bowls in a row on the counter like an assembly line

Note: Allow the kids to work their way down the line making their tacos in the way that they like.

Second Note: This is a messy meal so allow ample time for cleaning up.
—Laura W. Campbell

Thousand Island Taco Salad (H) (E)

Ingredients:

- 1 head iceberg lettuce
- 2 avocados
- 1 can chickpeas
- 1 can small black olives
- 1 lb ground turkey or beef
- 1 package taco seasoning
- 1 bottle thousand island dressing
- Shredded cheddar cheese
- Corn chips

Instructions:

1. Chop lettuce and avocados and put in large salad bowl.
2. Drain chicks and olives and add to salad.
3. Brown ground meat and follow instructions on seasoning packet.
4. Remove from heat and allow to cool for a few minutes.
5. Add bag of cheddar to top of salad and poor meat mixture over the top.
6. Add about ½ bottle of thousand island and toss until gooey.
7. Serve with crumbled corn chips over the top.

Note: Really amazing in the microwave on day 2. And 3.

—Kiva Schuler

Nestle Toll House Chocolate Chip Cookies (C) (E)

I baked these cookies every Wednesday when my children arrived back at my house for my custodial days. I always loved having the house smell like fresh baked cookies when they walked in the door.

Ingredients:

- Nestle Toll House Chocolate Chip Cookie Dough

Instructions:

1. Identify how many cookies you want to make, this can be anywhere from 2 - 24.
2. Determine how big you would like the cookies to be.
3. Scoop or slice cookie dough into your clean hands and mold into imperfect round balls.
4. Place 1-2 inches apart on the cookie sheet to allow for spreading when baked.
5. Bake at 350 for anywhere between 10 - 13 minutes depending on how crisp or doughy you would like them.

Note: Nestle now makes this mouthwatering cookie dough available in the old fashioned cylindrical tube, a flat bar with perforated squares and or a tub. All varieties work perfectly.

Second note: The dough is easier to work with when it is thawed but not quite room temperature. If it gets too warm it will begin sticking to your hands and become a pain in the ass to work with.

Third note: You can microwave cookies if you are only making 1 or 2 of them, but they will not get crispy at all. It will be like eating warm dough.

—*Laura W. Campbell*

Turkey Meatloaf (H) (C) (E)

Ingredients:

- Package of 95% lean ground turkey
- One full egg and one egg white
- Ketchup
- Salsa
- Breadcrumbs
- Mrs. Dash seasoning

Instructions:

1. Place the ground turkey in a large bowl.
2. Add full egg and egg white.
3. Add ketchup and salsa till the consistency of the mixture is soft but not too wet (about ½ cup of each).
4. Add breadcrumbs till the mixture is malleable and almost holds its shape.
5. Place the mixture into a bread/loaf pan.
6. Bake in 350 oven for about an hour or until cooked through.
7. Awesome served with mashed potatoes and peas.

—Laura W. Campbell

Vegetable Puree (H) (E)

Ingredients:

- 2 1/2 pounds fresh cauliflower florets, chopped
- 5 garlic cloves, sliced
- 1 ⅔ cups chicken broth
- 2 ½ teaspoons kosher salt
- 8 tablespoons almond milk
- 5 teaspoons butter

Instructions:

1. Place the cauliflower, garlic, chicken broth and salt in a large pot.
2. Bring to a boil.
3. Cover and reduce to medium heat. Simmer about 10 minutes or until the cauliflower is very tender.
4. Use an emulsion blender or transfer the pot contents to the bowl of a food processor fitted with a metal blade.
5. Add the almond milk and butter.
6. Process until smooth.
7. Season with black pepper.

Serves 6.

—Lisa Hodes

Vegetarian Chili (H) (C) (E)

Serves 6-8.

Ingredients:

- 3/4 c bulgar wheat
- 2 c. tomato juice
- 1/2 c. olive oil
- 2 c. chopped onion
- 3/4 c. chopped celery
- 1 c. chopped carrots
- 1 c. chopped green pepper
- 2 c. chopped mushrooms
- 2 c. chopped tomatoes (canned ok)
- 20 oz. can kidney beans
- 1 tsp. minced garlic
- 1/4 tsp. crushed red pepper
- 1 T. ground cumin
- 3 T. green chilies (can)

- 3 tsp. dried basil
- 3 tsp. oregano
- 1 or 2 T. chile power (to taste)
- 1 tsp. salt
- 2 T. lemon
- 3 T. Worcestershire sauce
- 1/2 tsp. Tabasco
- 1/4 c. dry white wine

Instructions:

1. Combine bulgar wheat and tomato juice and let soak.
2. In a large pot or skillet, heat olive oil over high heat, add onions, celery, green pepper, carrots, garlic and mushrooms.
3. Cook and stir 1-2 minutes.
4. Add bulgar wheat, tomato juice and all other ingredients.
5. Bring to a boil, reduce to a simmer and cook 30 minutes, uncovered.
6. Serve with rice.

Note: Not only delicious, but also therapeutic: Lots of chopping!

—Lisa Hodes

About us

Steve Kane

Married 1993. Separated 2015. Divorced 2016. Two wonderful sons.

When I was young my parents told me, *You can do anything you set your mind to.* Crazy me, I believed them. As a result I've had a crazy-quilt path, full of twists and turns, success and failure, very high highs, and very low lows. I've been a dishwasher and CEO, newspaper editor and video artist with work in museum shows, professionally written software, screenplays and haiku, been a music video producer and book store clerk. As a caterer, I was publicly dressed down by Robert De Niro; as a startup founder I was profiled by the *New York Times*. I have friends who are gazillionaire finance wizards, TV stars, and renowned physicians and scientists, as well as starving brilliant artists, street musicians, and failed impresarios one step ahead of the IRS. Plus, of course, many great friends who are just awesome humans, living normal, mostly-happy lives.

My resume and such, are online:

Social media

- Facebook: facebook.com/kane.steven
- Twitter: @stevenkane
- Instagram: @stevenkaneboston
- Snapchat: steven-kane
- LinkedIn: linkedin.com/in/kanesteven

Advisory Board

Laura W. Campbell
Executive Leadership Coach
Divorce Consultant
Author, *The Ultimate Divorce Organizer* -
http://amzn.to/2DimxBv
laurawcampbell.com

Jerry Colonna
CoFounder & CEO, Reboot.io
Certified Life Coach
Former Managing Director, J.P. Morgan and Flatiron Partners
Reboot.io

Lisa Hodes
Certified Divorce Coach
Former Family Law Attorney
lisahodes.com

Kiva Schuler
Founder & CEO, The Heartful Business
Certified Life Coach
CoFounder, The Wise Women Network
theheartfulbusiness.com

Credits

Website Design
The Heartful Business
theheartfulbusiness.com

Videography
Seacoast Flash
seacoastflash.com

Audio Production
Jack Kane
jackkanebeats.com

Personal Assessment Design & Production
DelfiNet
delfi-net.com

Please visit us at

GetHappy.Life